# UNFRIENDLY SKIES

# UNFRIENDLY SKIES

## Revelations of
## a Deregulated Airline Pilot

CAPTAIN **"X"** and Reynolds Dodson

**DOUBLEDAY**

New York   London   Toronto   Sydney   Auckland

**PUBLISHED BY DOUBLEDAY**
a division of Bantam Doubleday Dell Publishing Group, Inc.
666 Fifth Avenue, New York, New York 10103

DOUBLEDAY and the portrayal of an anchor with a dolphin
are trademarks of Doubleday, a division of
Bantam Doubleday Dell Publishing Group, Inc.

# Contents

# Preface

A licensed air transport pilot is in a precarious position. By law, the disclosure of any error—no matter how ancient, and no matter how unavoidable —can result in disciplinary action. There is no statute of limitations, and there are few avenues through which a pilot can appeal.

This may be one reason we have seen so few books written by pilots still active at major airlines.

That Captain "X" is a fine pilot will not be doubted. He does not inflate his abilities, and he does not pretend that he is omniscient. A man does not rise to the top of his profession, as Captain "X" has, by trading on delusion and self-congratulation.

But as a pilot, he has had to make judgments. That his judgments were correct has been substantiated by his clean record and by the many promotions he has received during his career. Nevertheless, some of his judgments might be used against him in the unpredictable court of peer opinion. Like the planes they fly, the people in Captain "X's" world are quick, fast-moving, and very demanding. They can also, like jets, be unforgiving.

The identity of Captain "X's" airline is irrelevant. This is a book about an industry, not a particular airline. Nevertheless, cities, airports, and route structures have been changed whenever the stories involve Captain "X's" personal experiences and the reputation of the line he serves. Where

Captain "X" was not personally involved, names, places, and dates are real, and the events were either recounted by the participants or else are a matter of public record.

Our procedure was simple. Captain "X" spoke, and I wrote. Occasionally, to give the reader a more rounded view, I sought additional information. I brought my research back to Captain "X," and we discussed it. Usually he would agree with what I had found, filtering it through the screen of his own unique experiences and giving it the flavor and tone that permeate this narrative. Occasionally I would dig up viewpoints and opinions with which he disagreed. In those instances, I always deferred to Captain "X."

To list everyone who helped behind the scenes with this project would be impossible. There is not a major airline that was not contacted, and there is hardly a department within the FAA or NTSB that did not provide some statistic, anecdote, insight, or opinion. Nevertheless, several people must suffer the embarrassment of being singled out.

The air traffic control sections could not have been written without the help of Pete Nelson, Manager of Public Affairs and Planning Staff for the Eastern Region of the FAA. Pete, with staffers Kathleen Bergen and Ben Kocivar, provided us with an inside look at air traffic control that is beyond the scope of the working airline pilot. I only hope we have managed to do well by them.

John Braden of the Airport Commissioner's Office in Atlanta was indefatigable in providing material on the operations at Hartsfield International.

John Mazor and Captain John O'Brien of the Airline Pilots Association were most helpful with the political sections and in reviewing certain passages which we deemed controversial.

Sam Saint, retired captain of American Airlines, lent his perspective to the problems of windshear and microbursts and the fate of Flight 191 in Dallas.

Tony Willett and the technicians of the FAA Technical Center provided a goodly portion of the technical, weather, and safety material.

Captain Roy Butler and the people at Pan Am's Flight Academy in Miami gave unstintingly of their time and advice on the various sections dealing with passenger service and emergency proceedings.

USAF Brigadier General (Ret.) George Cole of Tucson and Tom Swanton of the Pima Air Museum were most helpful as tour guides of the "desert boneyard."

Other contributors, such as Captain Reese Douglas Loftin of Delta,

Officer Charles Troyer of the Anne Arundel Police Department, Dr. Theodore Fujita of the University of Chicago, and Captain Homer Mouden, retired Manager of Flight Safety of Eastern Airlines, are mentioned within the body of the work, but will probably survive if they are thanked again here.

Reynolds Dodson
New York, 1989

## Why I Want to Be a Pilot

I want to be a pilot when I grow up because it's a fun job and easy to do. That's why there are so many pilots flying around today.

Pilots don't need much school, they just have to learn to read numbers so they can read instruments. I guess they should be able to read road maps so they can find their way if they get lost.

Pilots should be brave so they won't be scared if it's foggy and they can't see, or if a wing or motor falls off, they should stay calm. Pilots have to have good eyes to see through clouds, and they can't be afraid of lightening or thunder because they're closer to them than we are.

The salry pilots make is another thing I like. They make more money than they can spend. This is because most people think plane flying is dangerous, except pilots don't because they know how easy it is.

There isn't much I don't like, except that girls like pilots and all the stewardesses want to marry pilots so they always have to chase them away so they won't bother them.

I hope I don't get airsick because I get carsick and if I get airsick I couldn't be a pilot and then I'd have to go to work.

—Essay by a ten-year-old boy

# UNFRIENDLY SKIES

## Chapter 1

# **M**r. Spock

It should have been routine.

We were bringing a 727 into Saginaw, Michigan.* The weather was clear, and we had already begun our descent. I could see the airport spread out below me in a little geometric spill among the snowbanks.

In one of those boardroom maneuvers that's become endemic in our industry, my company had recently merged with a smaller airline. This had given us some new and, to me, unfamiliar routes. I had never been to Saginaw. I had spent the past several years flying DC-9s and 10s along the southern tier, and although I knew about 200 U.S. airports like the palm of my hand, this particular field was not among them.

On coming aboard I had introduced myself to the crew members. My copilot and my flight engineer were both new to me. They were employees of the now-absorbed smaller airline. My flight engineer looked eager. Like all flight engineers, he undoubtedly hoped someday to move into the copilot's seat, and from there into the captain's seat where I was sitting. My copilot was a man of about my age. I was forty-two.

Saginaw was the second leg of our trip. The flight had originated in

---

* Not the true location. Where necessary, airports and locales have been changed to protect the author and his airline.

Miami, and, following the custom of our industry, I had turned the controls over to the copilot after the first leg. During our preflight checkout I had asked him how long he had been driving the Seven-Two.

"Eight years," he said as he busied himself with the hundreds of minute details that go into every preflight checklist.

Eight years, I said to myself. That's pretty good.

While I was qualified to fly the 727, I was not as comfortable on it as I might have been. My experience on it had been mostly of a training nature, and I was glad to have a man at my side who had been living with the plane on such an intimate basis.

"And you know Saginaw," I said.

"Been flying there since the day I joined the company," came the succinct and perhaps slightly smug reply.

Terrific. Superterrific.

Through Flight Control, we had learned that the airport was undergoing renovation. The longer of her two runways—about 6,800 feet—had been temporarily shortened. It was now about 5,500 feet, which was well within the requirements of a 727, but considerably short of the 7,000 or so feet that would be considered average.

Her second runway—Runway 18—was about 5,000 feet.

Now 5,000 feet on a 727 is cutting it pretty close. Technically the plane can land in shorter runway space, but unless you've been making your home in that cockpit for quite a while you really don't want to go around testing a plane's minimum landing requirements.

As we neared our destination, air traffic control was reporting a twenty-five-knot headwind on Runway 18. This was significant. A strong headwind would greatly reduce ground speed, slowing the plane to a velocity acceptable to the shorter runway space.

"How do you plan to take her in?" I asked. (As captain, I'm the copilot's chief and mentor. From gate to gate, no matter who is actually handling the controls, everything that happens is the captain's responsibility.)

"Runway 18," he said. "I'll bring her in at a forty flap."

As you might imagine, a plane's flap setting is crucial to the landing procedure. The farther the flaps are down, the lower the nose is tilted. It's what we call the *deck angle*. The usual flap setting—the one I had been performing day in and day out along the southern tier—is thirty degrees. By choosing a forty-degree setting, my copilot was indicating that he was planning to alter our deck angle, augment the amount of "drag" (resistance of air as it flows across the wings), and take advantage of the headwind to lessen our velocity. These factors would enable us to land the plane at a relatively slow 120 knots and come to a stop well within the 5,000-foot limit.

"Good decision," I said.

As a passenger, you've probably applauded when the pilot brings the plane in on one of those smooth-as-glass, I-hardly-even-felt-us-touch-the-ground grease jobs. From where you sit, there's no greater testimony to your pilot's skill than that he didn't ruffle your in-flight reading matter. That's great. But what you don't know is that sometimes those ultra-smooth landings can kill you. If the weather is bad . . . if there's just a little too much ice out there on the tarmac . . . if the runway is too slick, or too short, or too sloped, or too *any*thing, sometimes the *right* decision is to bring that plane down, cut your forward momentum to a crawl, and *slam* the wheels onto the pavement. That way you'll get full braking power and diminish the risk of skidding or hydroplaning.

That's the *right* decision.

Which is not to say it's the greatest crowd-pleaser.

In this case, it took me about half a second to conclude that my copilot was making an absolutely 100 percent *right* decision, and once again I congratulated myself on having the good fortune to draw Mr. Spock as my first officer.

So there I sat, ignorant and blissful, my arms folded across my chest, my Coke and my peanuts at my side, 152 equally ignorant and blissful passengers in the cabin behind me, and none of us having the faintest idea we had about ninety-seven seconds to live.

One of the great thrills of flying is that you're constantly getting to experience what other men spend their entire lives clawing and scratching to achieve—namely, that awe-inspiring, ego-swelling phenomenon called "The View from the Fortieth Floor." I never tire of it. The landscape is constantly changing. As I crisscross the country, I marvel at what most other people get to see only a relatively few times in their lives. I wouldn't trade offices with Donald Trump on a bet.

But when you're coming in for that delicate operation called the land-ing, "The View from the Fortieth Floor" takes on a special significance. You're not sitting in an office with your feet up on the desk, you're sitting at the tip of a very fast and very powerful falling arrow. Your decisions are crucial. You're scanning your instrument panel. You're making numerous small adjustments in your ailerons and your elevators. You're watching to see that your wings are level, your airspeed's steady, your landing gear's down, your attitude's proper. And while you're doing all that, and while you're looking at your engine pressure and your compass headings and your rate of descent and your altitude gauges, you're also looking through your windshield and you're comparing what you're seeing on the ground with what you've seen a thousand times before in a thousand other similar landings. It's all very fast, and very instinctive. Only when the airport is new to you; when the terrain is just a little different from any you've ever seen before; when it's a plane you're not quite comfortable with, and it's coming in on a configuration that is almost never used except in the most unusual circumstances, sometimes then your instincts don't work right. You sit there and you stare and you realize that all your exhaustive training has not prepared you for the unique and somewhat confusing sensations you're actually experiencing. And when that happens, all you can do is marvel at what a weird and unsettling feeling this is, and you look for support in your copilot's competence.

As I sat there, I couldn't help thinking, Now isn't this strange? As many times as I've looked at runways through these windshields . . . as many hours as I've spent training on a Seven-Two and lifting her off and setting her down and going through God-knows-how-many exercises and emergency training procedures with her, isn't it strange how, when you come in at this steep angle toward a runway you've never seen before, you have the optical illusion you're about to crash?

I rolled a peanut over on my tongue.

The ground rose closer.

And isn't it strange, I thought, the way it looks like you may not even clear those trees down there, but even if you do clear those trees you're certainly going to hit those lights, and aren't you lucky that Mr. Spock here knows so much more than you, and that the lump rising in your throat, which seems to be getting larger with every passing moment, is apparently not rising in his much more knowledgeable one?

In twenty years of service, I've listened to more than my share of dead men's chatter on voice recorders. I've sat through more than my share of postcrash conferences and listened to more than my share of ghostly conversations coming from those charred and battered "black boxes." And I know that the last word a pilot often utters before his plane disappears in a fiery ball of flame is *shit.* That may not be a very noble way to depart this planet, but that's the way we usually exit.

I can't swear that that particular Anglo-Saxonism was the one that escaped my lips at that moment, but if it wasn't, it wasn't for lack of thinking it.

Snapping forward, I grabbed the yoke with one hand and pushed the throttle forward with the other. We were a good hundred yards short of the runway, and we were doomed to crash.

Looking back on it now, I realize how silly it was. I realize how foolish I was to have placed so much confidence in a man I didn't know and whose only collateral was his self-assured arrogance. The group dynamics of cockpit crew members are pivotal to the success or failure of every flight, and it is just this kind of misunderstanding that can snuff out lives in a fraction of a second. But I didn't have the luxury of thinking about all that at that moment. There was the ground, here came the airplane, and all I could do was to act reflexively.

*"Power . . . full power!"* I cried.

I knew that my only chance, if I had a chance, was to bring the nose up, push the throttles to the limit, and hope like hell we would clear those approach lights. Straining forward against my shoulder harness, I slammed the throttles against the firewall.

The plane leaped forward.

I won't even venture to guess what the passengers must have thought at that moment. Even through the closed cockpit door I could hear the first of what would be many crashes as dirty food trays, coffeepots, and various pieces of overhead baggage shifted violently in their compartments. Within microseconds the airspeed indicator shot from 122 to 143 knots. The plane bolted, flared—then hit the pavement.

Later inspection would show that our main gear had cleared the end of the runway by less than thirty inches. A pilot is trained to land a plane within the first thousand feet of runway space. Landing it within the first thirty inches of runway space is cutting it just a little closer than the company that owns the airplane might wish.

But that wasn't the bad part. The bad part—the part that would bring my heart almost literally into my throat and make me wonder how my mother's little boy had ever come to be in this predicament—was that we were now hurtling down a dwarf-sized runway at a speed approximating a Grand Prix race car's!

As any pilot will tell you, when you have executed a landing as sloppy and screwed-up as this one, there is only one right thing to do. The right thing to do is keep the throttle shoved forward, lift the plane back off the ground, and execute what's called a "go-around." It's an inelegant and rather embarrassing maneuver, but it's the one the experts consider most prudent.

And the experts are right.

Unfortunately, that is not the procedure my reflexes chose to perform.

The procedure my reflexes chose was to cut the throttle, reverse the engine thrust, raise the spoilers (those are the big noisy flaps on the tops of the wings), and apply the brakes. In other words, in the split-second's confusion caused by the poorly planned landing, my instincts overrode my training—and I decided to *stop the goddamn airplane!*

If you think the crashes in the cabin were bad before, you should have heard the outlandish noises coming from that quarter now. Everything that was not nailed down in the galley flew against the forward bulkhead. Along the aisle, the overhead compartments began springing open, *pop, pop, pop,* showering overcoats, garment bags, pillows, blankets, you name it, onto the hapless heads of the people below them. All the oxygen masks came down. These masks are held in place by barometric latches which release during pressure changes. The reactionary force of our landing had pulled the pins, and now there were a hundred-and-some-odd oxygen masks and hoses dangling before the bewildered and panic-stricken eyes of our whiplashed passengers.

Still the plane roared on.

I sat clench-jawed at the controls. I could see the end of the runway rising up before me. The plane was skipping and skidding along the pavement, its tires alternately grabbing and sliding as we heaved and rattled across the asphalt. My feet were pressed as hard as they would go against the brake pedals. In another few seconds the plane would nosedive off the far end of the runway, slide along the ground on its belly, and end up in the same fiery inferno we had so narrowly averted at the runway's near end.

God have mercy on us all.

The fact that that didn't happen is, to me, still a bit of a miracle. Somehow the combined forces of brakes and spoilers and Lady Luck managed to slow our momentum, and the plane, after no small amount of protest, shuddered to a halt. We were sitting with our nose practically overhanging the end of the runway, but we were breathing.

The next few minutes are unclear. Somehow I managed to get the plane turned around and taxied toward the gate. Somehow I managed to get the switches off and the knobs turned and the levers pulled and the engines shut down. Somehow the ground crew managed to get the stairs rolled over to the passenger door, the cabin crew managed to get the passenger door open, and those poor scared passengers managed to crawl out of the Valley of Death and into the lap of sweet terra firma. *("Thanks for flying with us, and we do hope you'll choose us again the next time you travel!")*

The three of us in the cockpit sat there white-faced. For the next couple of minutes you could hear a pin drop. Finally—softly, and as offhandedly as possible—I suggested that the flight engineer might want to go out and get a cup of coffee.

"Roger!" said the flight engineer, and you've never seen a man exit a cockpit door as fast as that one did.

This left just me and Mr. Spock.

"I will try to put this as kindly and succinctly as I can," I said. "Just what the bloody fuck did you think you were doing back there? Just what the bloody fuck did you, in your eight distinguished years of flying Seven-Twos, mean by coming in on such an erroneous and obviously half-assed approach angle? Didn't you see we were about to crash? Didn't you in your infinite wisdom see that that was completely the wrong sight picture we were getting through the windshield, and that we were all about two seconds away from becoming crispy critters on this North Woods landscape?"

Mr. Spock squirmed uncomfortably.

I won't belabor this poor fellow's humiliation. Suffice it to say that it was as sincere as it was deserved. Suffice it also to say that when the dust had settled, not to mention my pulse rate, I learned that everything he had told me during our preflight checkout was true. He *had* been flying 727s for eight years. He *had* been coming into the Saginaw airport since the day he joined his company. As a *flight engineer!* This was only his third trip as a copilot! He had never actually *landed* a plane at Saginaw, and he had never made a forty-flap landing in his life!

In the years since, I've had a lot of time to think about that incident. I've awakened in the middle of the night, and I can still see the end of that runway racing toward me like some ghostly image from Christmas Future. And it never ceases to impress me that, had we crashed, the report issued by the National Transportation Safety Board would have attributed the carnage to "pilot error." About seven out of ten airline accidents in this country are labeled that way, and this, most assuredly, would have been one of them.

But as someone once wrote, "Most pilot errors are not really pilot errors so much as booby traps that the pilot has fallen into." Indeed, "pilot error" is itself an error. That pilots are human and make mistakes is self-evident; but there are reasons for those mistakes, and those are the factors which must be examined.

Let's take another look at that incident, and this time let's see it for what it really was:

*Factor 1: Both my copilot and my flight engineer were new to me.*

This in and of itself is not unusual. The airline I work for has more than 5,000 assorted pilots, copilots, and flight engineers. It is not unlikely that I am going to have many strangers share my flight deck as we sail about the world from this city to that.

What is worth noting is that, before deregulation, I could usually assume that my associates were competent. Since we worked for the same company, we had probably been hired with the same criteria in mind; we had gone through the same academic and practical exercises; and we were subject to the same corporate objectives and operations guidelines.

We were a *team*.

Since deregulation, there have been dozens of mergers involving hundreds of air routes and many thousands of disconsolate employees. This means that on a significant number of flights part of the crew will have been trained on one airline, part on another. Many of today's crew members come from small airlines who have neither the money nor the equipment to give them the sophisticated jet training they need. The result can be disastrous.

This was shown on a snowy afternoon in November 1987. That was the day a Continental DC-9 tipped a wing on takeoff from Denver's Stapleton Airport and flipped over, strewing bodies, glass, and twisted debris along a thousand feet of windswept runway. Twenty-eight of the eighty-two people on board were killed. Subsequent investigation showed that the captain had spent a mere thirty-three hours in the airplane's captain's seat. His first officer, who was at the controls at the time, had been hired a couple of months earlier from a small commuter airline in Texas. He had flown a DC-9 on only one previous scheduled flight, and he had never taken off in snow. This may not have been the most *immediate* cause of this accident (accidents are almost always the result of a series of errors, misjudgments, flukes, and coincidences), but the unfortunate pairing of these two men was undoubtedly a factor that helped to precipitate it.

In my case, the only information I had about my copilot was that he had been "flying" a 727 for a considerable length of time. It never occurred to me to question his definition of "flying." Nor did I doubt his meaning when he said that he had been landing planes in Saginaw since the day he joined the company. In retrospect, I can see how the misunderstanding arose. I can assure you that I have been much more careful in my questioning of copilots since that incident, but at the time that it happened it had just never occurred to me, and the fact that it didn't almost cost us all dearly.

*Factor 2: I, as captain, didn't know the airport.*

Before deregulation, when a crew took off in an airplane, there was at least a pretty good chance that the place they were going was familiar to one or more of the crew members. Because the industry was so controlled, air routes were fairly static. A pilot for, say, Piedmont knew the Southern and Mid-Atlantic areas like the back of his hand. He didn't have to wake up one morning and start worrying about thunderstorms in Dallas/Fort Worth or the Chinook winds that whip the Rockies.

Today it's different. Our schedules are so rushed, the economics of flying are so tight, the distances we travel are so great, that we often find ourselves caroming this way and that like so many billiard balls around a pool table. To take but one example: In the twelve-month period that included Texas Air's now famous merger binge (that's the period when Continental was merged with Eastern, Frontier, People Express, and New York Air), that one company alone added 177 new cities to its route structure. At the same time it shuffled some 61,000 employees, including approximately 8,000 pilots and copilots. You can imagine the chaos. While many of the pilots may have known many of the airports they now had to serve, it was not unusual for a pilot from one airline to be teamed with a copilot from another, and the two of them sent off to some hell-and-gone airport neither one of them had ever seen before.

That's a formula for disaster.

Pilots don't like to admit that this is a problem. Every pilot likes to think that, as a professional, he can handle any new circumstance as it arises. But I can tell you from personal experience: not knowing an airport, or not knowing a geographical or meteorological area through which you have to fly in order to reach that airport, is one more factor that can lead to misjudgment.

*Factor 3: The copilot and I were about the same age.*

In commercial aviation, flight crews advance in one way and one way only: seniority. When you are hired, your name goes on at the bottom of a list. From that moment on your career will consist of climbing that list one number at a time. You will climb it first as a flight engineer, then as a first officer, and finally as a captain. That's the way it has always been, and that's the way it will probably always be.

Unfortunately, the seniority track at one airline may be quite different from the seniority track at another. If your airline is financially unhealthy —if it is poorly managed, or if it is caught between the price-slashing big guys and the aggressive commuters—your chances for advancement are nil. I know many highly capable men—men who have just as much commercial flight time as I do, and probably a great deal more military flight time—who, even after fifteen or twenty years, are still flying as flight engineers or copilots. It's not their fault, it's just the luck of the draw. Those who in their youth were fortunate enough to link up with a well-managed company with growth potential have made out okay. Those who weren't— too bad.

Looking back on it, I'm convinced that this "unevenness" of seniority contributed to our near-disaster in Saginaw. I had been with my airline thirteen years. My airline was healthy, and I had long been a captain. My copilot had been with his airline twelve years, and he had barely made it past flight engineer. What could be more natural than his not wanting to admit—to me, of all people—that he had never actually landed in Saginaw?

It's been said that a pilot's ego is exceeded only by the size of his wristwatch. In this case, my copilot's ego (ably abetted by my own complacency) almost killed us.

Of course deregulation isn't the only thing that keeps things jumping in the airplane business nowadays. Flying one of today's new jets—an MD-80, say, or a 767—verges on something out of "Star Trek." Since my brush with fate in Michigan, I've flown 727s, 737s and 747s, and now I fly the near-state-of-the-art 767s almost exclusively. I'm one of a fairly select number of pilots who's qualified to do so. And my experiences on these planes—my run-ins with passengers, my relations with stewardesses, my tangles with weather and crazies and security problems—are probably enough to fill a book.

In fact, they *are* enough to fill a book. This book.

The question is, Where to begin?

Well, there's an old saying in our industry: When an air traveler dies, it makes no difference whether he's going to heaven or hell. Either way (come on, you know this) . . . either way, he has to change in Atlanta.

# Chapter 2

# Airport '88

I've been flying through Atlanta for about the past twenty years or so. I've watched this field grow into one of the world's transportation capitals. There have been times during those years when it looked like a strip-mining operation. Whole mountains of earth would spring up, and then get leveled again.

O'Hare serves more people. La Guardia has more traffic congestion. Dallas/Ft. Worth covers a great deal more acreage. But Atlanta is biggest in terms of overall flight operations, and it is by far the most advanced in both its design and in its passenger handling.

The history of our business is, on the whole, rather checkered. It's a boom-or-bust story full of tycoons and mail route struggles. Most of the carriers—or at least the ones with some years behind them—have had "point to point" contracts through the main population centers. But in the early 1940s something interesting happened. Some of these carriers began to sprout what are called "feeder routes." Instead of flying point to point, they'd pick a "hub" and add "spokes" to it. Atlanta's Hartsfield Airport became the first of these intersections.

When the lines were deregulated—this was in the late 1970s now—the need for cost effectiveness became more and more obvious. Suddenly it was noticed that the firms that had hub structures made considerably more

11

money than those that had linear operations. The reason, of course, had to do with the traffic patterns. By establishing a hub you could dominate an area better. Your maintenance equipment, not to mention your airplanes, could be kept in one place rather than being strewn around the countryside.

Hartsfield International actually began as a racetrack oval. In 1911 Barney Oldfield drove roadsters here. In the decade to come it saw occasional car rallies and was frequently used for various air shows and stunt performances. But it wasn't too long before it had become a regional air center. By the early 1930s it had become a nexus for Eastern. By the mid-1980s, thanks to the growth of the sunbelt, it was vying with O'Hare for the Number-One Airport title.

I want to take you on a tour through this incredible work complex. I want to show you some things that are rarely seen by the flying public. By the time we get through you'll know a little about airports—and you'll certainly know more about why flying is so hectic nowadays.

Let's begin with the runways. As the planes approach touchdown, they'll be looking at runways which extend latitudinally. There are four altogether, each with numbers and letters on it. The numbers correspond to the points on an airplane compass.

Each of these strips is the width of five highway lanes. It's constructed on a subbase of gravel and concrete. There's a sixteen-inch layer of cement with steel mesh inside of it that's been spread out on top and stretches 8,000 feet or longer.

At old-fashioned fields you'll see runways and cross-runways. The cross-runways are there in order to accommodate wind directions. At a field like O'Hare there are at least half a dozen runways, but if you tried to use them all you'd have one hell of a collision out there.

At a field like Atlanta's, none of the strips intersect each other. The planes we have now can handle most moderate wind anomalies. So the planes that are landing are never delayed by departing flights. There's a constant rotation. It's like a perpetual motion machine.

A glance at the statistics shows the virtues of this field design. Unlike O'Hare (or even Dallas/Ft. Worth, for that matter) Hartsfield can boast, at least at the time of this writing, that they have never had an accident that's resulted in a passenger fatality. That is why designers look to Hartsfield for construction concepts. The things you'll find here are on an elevated efficiency level. When a Denver or a Los Angeles goes to upgrade its airfield, it's here that it will look. Hartsfield was built for the deregulation era.

At the field's eastern edge you'll see a couple of *flight kitchens.* These are the caterers which prepare all those feasts we savor. They'll use linen for first class, paper for tourist class, and they'll pack it all up and truck it out to the airplane galleys. I've visited those kitchens. They're truly remarkable. They've got ovens in there that are the size of small semitrailers. They can roast 5,000 chickens in about thirty-five minutes, and their menus are designed by the best European culinary specialists.

Or at least that's what they tell me. Who am I to say they're exaggerating.

Nearby, closer in, are the cargo and baggage centers. Depending on the airline, these are highly sophisticated. Both Eastern and Delta, which handle most of the passengers here, use laser-guided scanners to facilitate sorting problems.

Here's how that works: They'll stick a tag on the bag you give them. The tag will have a code, similar to the bar codes on supermarket items. When it passes a scanner, the code is deciphered; the scanner notes its flight and its place on the conveyor belt order. A little farther on, there'll be a gauntlet of pusher-arms. Assuming your bag is, say, tenth on the conveyor belt, the machine tells the arms to push the tenth into the "Tucson" bin. As your bag passes "Tucson," it will be pushed into the "Tucson" container.

An airport this size has a number of fiefdoms in it. There are sections controlled by the various airline companies. Since 1941, this has been the Delta firm's headquarters, and they have a large corporate complex across the northernmost runway area. There's a Wildlife Department and a Drug Enforcement and a Customs office. There's a 100-man police force and a 135-man fire battalion. Like most larger fields, it has its own FBI contingent. A crime involving planes is not the same as a street infraction.

Parts of this field are under the control of the Commissioner's Office. The commissioner, in Atlanta, is funded by the community. You should remember this sometimes when you're complaining to an airline employee. It's possible that it's the mayor who's causing whatever your particular problem is.

Other airport areas are in the purview of Washington. The approach lights and the control tower are under the FAA's authority. This authority, in turn, is part of the Department of Transportation, which is a vast, sprawling bureau that includes railroad and highway operations.

As you walk around this field, which covers 3,750 acres and has 8 miles of runway and more than 3 miles of passenger concourse, you'll see 142 gates serving 38 airlines, and there will be about 170 planes either landing or departing hourly from them.

*One hundred and seventy planes.* Think about that. That comes to almost three planes a minute—more than any other airport in the history of aviation.

There's a post office here. They bring the mail in by conveyor belt. It will be dumped into bins that have various destinations attached to them. Each of these bins has an oversized scale attached, so that when it's taken to a plane they'll know exactly how much weight it represents. Weight, on a plane, is figured scientifically. The hold has to be filled to conform to certain weight-and-balance standards. There are even differing estimates for summer and winter flights: passengers in winter wear more clothes and bring more carry-ons with them.

You'll see cargo operations. They have sixteen strictly freight lines here. Most of that traffic operates in the o'dark-thirty hours. They'll move many thousands of tons, including produce and chemicals, and you'll see everything pass through here from azaleas to zoo animals.

An airport this size is in itself a small metropolis. The characters you'll meet can range from drug smugglers to Hare Krishna zealots. As you stroll through the terminal, you'll see millionaires and pickpockets, and there are a hundred-and-some-odd shops that have literally millions of dollars' worth of merchandise moving through them.

The terminal itself is the size of twelve football fields. There's an escalator here that takes you down to a "transportation mall." There, a rubber-tired subway whisks you off to four concourses, while a computerized voice warns you to "step back, the doors are closing."

On any given day, you'll see 140,000 people here. There are another 40,000 who call Hartsfield their business address. Hartsfield International is one of the Southeast's greatest resources, pumping some $7 billion a year into the local economic structure.

I remember one morning, I was about to take off from here. I had just passed security and was walking out toward the passenger gate. I happened to look down toward where the plane was being loaded and I saw this—what—all this *stuff.* It was spilling out onto the tarmac area.

I just stood there. I watched it. I thought maybe it was . . . *toilet water?* I thought maybe there was a leak in one of our fore or aft lavatories. It seemed to be gushing from the bottom of the airplane. It was running down the wheels and along the ground, where a truck stood idling.

I continued to walk. My mind was preoccupied. A strong, pungent smell seemed to waft through the passenger gate. I couldn't for the life of me figure what could be leaking, and it was several more seconds before the logic intruded on me.

*"Holy Jesus!"* I muttered.

I clutched at my flight case. I broke into a run, and I pushed past some passengers. I grabbed at a stewardess who was standing on the airplane, and I cried, "Everybody off!" and I began hurredly evacuating them.

As I later found out, it had been caused by a cargo truck. The truck had swung wide to make way for a baggage carrier. The roof of the truck had made a crease in the airplane wing, rupturing the skin and spilling a tankful of fuel all over. Had a fire broken out the results would have been mind-boggling. The fuel in these planes isn't as explosive as gasoline, but it's enormously hot—it's a firefighter's nightmare—and had it managed to ignite, it would have been like getting hit by a napalm rocket.

I'm remembering this because it aims toward a point I'm making: You, as a passenger, worry mostly about altitude. *But the single worst place in a jet airplane's work cycle is not in the air, it's right here on this apron area.*

You don't believe that? Come, I'll show you a ramp tower. On the roof of each concourse is a square, glassed-in ramp tower. When a flight gets assembled, it's like the pieces of a jigsaw puzzle. Up there, in those towers, is where it all comes together somehow.

Up here, looking down, you'll see what looks like an ant colony. There will be many rows of planes. They'll all be parked beside the passenger gates. They'll be nuzzled, snout first, like huge fish at a fish-feeder, surrounded by men who are either loading them or repairing something on them. Ten years ago, all those aprons were manageable. They were busy but sane. The lines were still regulated. No one had to worry about the tightness of their schedules or the time it might take to get a plane up and flying again. Now it's all different. Today it's frenetic down there. You've got passengers to load. You've got maintenance and fuel deliveries. A plane on the ground is a plane losing money, and you either move it, by God, or you'll have your board of directors growling at you.

If you're an airline maven, and you've been studying the news accounts, and you've been reading all those stories of what goes on at the ticket counters, you're probably aware of how, at airports like Stapleton, both United and Continental are practically shanghaiing passengers from each other. Well, that's how it is now. And it's spread to the ramp areas. I've seen pilots from one airline purposely roadblock another airline. I've seen the taxiway equivalent of chicken and drag racing in which planes ace each other in an attempt to move up in the takeoff order.

There's a story they tell. I think this happened in Florida somewhere. There was a 727, and it cut in front of an L-1011. The Lockheed had been first, but the controller didn't protest. He let the 727 keep its place in the takeoff order.

"How 'bout that!" could be heard coming over the radio from the 727's obviously rather pleased-with-himself captain.

The 727 continued to move toward the runway. The Lockheed pilot, up until now, had said nothing. The three-engine Boeing slowly turned and stood waiting. Clearance was given, and it began to initiate its takeoff procedure.

As the 727 began to roll down the runway, the Lockheed captain pushed the button on his microphone. He snuggled the mike against the speaker of his emergency system, then he flicked the "test" switch. There was a god-awful warning honker.

*"Christ!"* cried the Boeing captain as his plane lifted skyward. His ears were practically splitting from the sound of the emergency warning. As they staggered into the air, they could hear the voice of the Lockheed pilot. It was as smooth as smooth silk.

"How 'bout *that,*" it was saying to them.

This same cutthroat spirit even extends to the flight kitchens. Here at Hartsfield International there's a Marriott and a Dobbs House kitchen. They'll cook 100,000 dinners for a day's load of passenger-diners, and their safe operation is of paramount importance to us. But talk to either one, they'll tell you the other's untrustworthy: their workers are miserable; their kitchen is unsanitary; their drivers and loaders are all drunk or mani-acal, and you shouldn't eat their food because it's probably got rat turds mixed in it.

Such slurs give one pause. You begin to feel a bit paranoid. You go across the field and you talk to some baggage handlers. They regale you with stories of what American did to them, or how Delta acts arrogant, or how Eastern's too union-laden. It's like a hundred little enclaves—and it's hurting our safety record. In 1986 (the latest figures available to me) there were about 500 accidents on U.S. domestic ramp areas, which is about 80 percent more than the 1982 figures.

It was not always thus. Hell, it used to be friendly here. If a Braniff got canceled, they'd send you over to . . . well, Northwest, possibly; and Northwest would help you: they'd put you on an airplane, and the overall result would be a boost for the airline industry. Well, now they'll do that—they'll send you over to a competitor. Only they'll conveniently "forget" and leave your bags out on a loading platform. Since the final-leg carrier is responsible for the luggage delivery, it'll be the connecting line, Northwest, that will have both passengers and government barking at them.

It's this sort of thing that's beginning to make us all nervous nowadays. There was a poll taken recently in which they surveyed some airline pilots. About one out of three said that their job was more perilous, and more than 50 percent thought that their work was more stressful nowadays. I'm in that vote-bloc. There have been charges of maintenance shortcuts. I've not seen that—my line's acted responsibly (thank God!)—but it certainly is true that when you land at an airport nowadays you'll be sharing one mechanic, whereas you used to have several assigned to you.

Let me take a few minutes and try to sort out these maintenance issues. There was another recent poll—and this was taken in Atlanta, actually—showing that the majority of pilots thought their planes were less "airworthy." If you're an average airline passenger, this may not sound too pleasing to you.

What we're talking about here are not the make-or-break safety items. They are not the big items we call the "no-go," or "kill," items. What they are are small ailments which are ultimately important but which are not that essential to a particular day's flight operations. You'll find scratched and nicked panels. You'll find levers with knob-ends missing. You'll find fraying and chipping and rattling and lightbulbs missing. Ten years ago you would have gone and raised hell about it. Not so today. Today you'd be considered a "troublemaker."

Let me say here that, if you're looking for scapegoats—if you want to blame these problems on the unions, or on labor propaganda—the people who serve airlines are not your average jaded office workers: they have a light in their eyes you just don't see in more earthbound people. The guys at my airline wouldn't think of turning their uniforms in. They may gripe on occasion, but that's usually about all they'll do. In twenty years of flying I've seen very few career shifts. Even a guy who's working ground crew would have to be pushed beyond the breaking point.

And yet—

In 1987, due to problems with their management, more than seven hundred Eastern pilots simply handed in their notices. Seven hundred pilots! That was about a sixth of their workforce. And since it ended their seniority, it meant they had chucked their whole flying careers.

To me, this is a sign that something's wrong with the system somewhere. We've got all these great theories that have been concocted by economists, but we're trying to impose them on a hazardous environment where, when push comes to shove, there are going to be morale problems and injuries happening.

They've already happened. I heard this one from a friend of mine: The

captain of the plane was moving out toward the taxi area. He was maneuvering the plane between a couple of buildings when he saw a man on a
ladder working at a competitor's maintenance area. "Look at this," he told
his copilot. He pushed up one engine throttle. There was a huge roar of
flame. It was like the blast from a blast furnace. When the copilot looked
back, there was no man—there was no ladder even. They had blasted that
guy thirty yards across the apron area!

Now don't get me wrong—we aren't all a bunch of maniacs out there.
In twenty years of service I've seen very little sabotage. But I have no
qualms in saying that, despite our professionalism, the overall mood has
become more and more unsalutary. You yourself may have noticed. Take a
look around your airplane cabin. Your seat won't go back. You may find
ashtrays and head cloths missing. There used to be a time when we could
borrow parts from a competitor. Not anymore. You need a widget, you can
whistle for it.

You can't prove these points by simply reeling off accident statistics.
Accident statistics are notoriously untrustworthy. One big jumbo crash
will cause a spike in our accident graph, while a thousand near-misses are
virtually ignored by the headline writers.

What *can* be asserted is that we're eroding the "safety buffer." Our good
safety record has been the result of "overcautiousness." We've checked and
rechecked. We've left nothing to happenstance. We've pulled planes out of
line before the government even said we should.

Now, in tough times, we're cutting down on those safety margins. We
keep edging ever closer to the minimums expected of us. Whereas in the
days of regulation we checked everything and rechecked it, now we'll
check once. Or, worse, we'll put it on our *"mañana* list."

So as we clock in for duty, this is the world in which we find ourselves.
There's professionalism, yes—but there's also a cynicism. You can't help
suspecting that there's a shark in the aquarium. And what makes it even
worse—it's not even six in the morning yet.

# Chapter 3

# **P**reflight

It's five forty-five, and I've been up for an hour now. I've showered and shaved. I've put on my uniform. I've grabbed a quick roll over at the Harley just west of here, and I've hooked a ride in on one of that inn's hospitality limos.

The "rush hour" at Hartsfield begins about seven. Up until now it's been quiet. The sky looks like gun metal. In another few minutes, the planes will start swarming, and you'll see them descend like huge birds with their wing lights glowing.

It's been my observation that, when I'm talking to Earth People (my own appellation; I distinguish them from Airline People), the life that I'm leading seems to interest but puzzle them. The hours I keep . . . the adventure and the restlessness of it . . .

Let's talk about that. From an Earth Person's viewpoint, a man should be bound by the rules of geography. He's not supposed to float like some goddamn bacterium and feel strangely nostalgic for the decor of an airport corridor.

But that's how I am. Say you're sitting in Los Angeles. Say it's nine in the morning, and I'm calling you from Dallas. I say, "Let's get together," and you say, "Great, I'd enjoy that sometime," and I say, "No, I mean now. We'll grab a quick bite of lunch together."

19

That bothers people. They want their friends to be *anchored* somewhere. They want their friends to say, "Well . . . but there are 1,200 miles between us!" And those 1,200 miles are supposed to prove insurmountable, so that you can't just blow in and go blowing back out again. I've known guys who get furious. I'll tell them I'm flying somewhere. I'm going to Rome—I'm having lunch with a stewardess there—then I'm off to Nairobi, I'll be doing some mountain climbing, then I'm going to Cancun for a couple of days scuba diving. Talk about pissed! Some of these people get livid with me! I can *hear* their throats tighten. I can *feel* their eyes narrowing. And they'll say, "Oh." Just like that. As in, "Oh. Well, fuck *you,* you bastard," and they'll spend all night sulking, and there'll be no way of mollifying them.

Occasionally I'll meet a friend I haven't seen in a year or two. He'll say, "Hey, man, what's new!" and I'll be foolish enough to tell him. To a pilot, "what's new" often spans several continents. It involves thunder and lightning, and it will have adventure and often sex wrapped up in it.

This is not to imply that we're all Indiana Joneses. Flying a plane involves a certain amount of tedium. There are many long hours spent scanning the horizon and engaging in talk with someone who may not be that interesting to you. But when people make remarks about my job being "boring". . . well, all I can say is that they've never been an airplane pilot. There is nothing ever boring about a takeoff or a landing, and there is certainly nothing boring about that ever-changing sky we fly through.

Another contention, if such one can call it, is that while everybody else is out and *working* for a living, I, as a pilot, will be sitting around loafing, and I'll be rewarded for that because it's FAA-mandated.

From the earliest days, back when planes were still barnstorming, it became obvious to science that flying took a lot out of you. The concentration required was so compressed, so intensified, that if you worked "normal" hours you'd be compromising safety standards.

So it was early decreed that we should work limited work-months. We work an eighty-hour month, which is about half of what an Earth Person labors. This gives us free time in which to moonlight, or visit people, or flirt with friends' wives, or lounge around clipping stock certificates.

There are many, many pilots who have jobs other than airline piloting. When they aren't in the air they'll be dealing in business franchises. They'll be real estate brokers, or they'll have law or MBA degrees. There was one guy I flew with who, on the ground, had a medical practice.

Of course when a pilot's actually flying he never refers to that as *working* at something. You'll never hear a pilot say he's "going to work" that morning. Flying isn't work. Flying is like breathing. You give a pilot a choice, he'll choose flying over sex, I daresay.

Although I wouldn't want to put that to a test if I were you.

In exchange for such pleasures, there are a number of "dues" required of us. We have to spend many nights in some anonymous motel room somewhere. We get up in the dark, we fumble around with our suitcases, and we have to try to pick clothes that will work in all temperature ranges.

We're always getting colds. We're never certain what hour it is. In twenty years of flying, I've given up keeping my wristwatch current. Unless I'm in a city for at least a half-week or longer, I don't bother to change it. I just keep it on Central Time.

In addition to that, we have a number of professional burdens. We're constantly reviewed, both by our companies and by our government overseers. There is no other profession—and that certainly includes medicine—which is so carefully scrutinized and so dependent upon peer evaluation.

A little later on, I'll take you up for a simulator ride. Most of our training is performed on a simulator nowadays. These are replicated cockpits that are kept at our training schools and whose computer-driven programs can virtually duplicate flying conditions. All airline pilots learn their skills on a simulator. Even Third World pilots come to America for simulator training. There's a very good chance that when you get on an airplane nowadays, your junior-most officers will have had nothing but simulator training.

But of course when you're hired you've already got your pilot's license. If you're a military pilot, you'll have several thousand hours behind you. That will look good on your job application form, but you'll have to start at the bottom and learn from scratch how an airliner operates.

"Promotion," in our business, isn't the same as in other businesses. I've already mentioned the importance of seniority. Seniority is a determinant of your pay and of the schedules you get. It's also a criterion for who gets first crack at a job opening.

There's also "advancement" by plane type and route structure. A jumbo-jet captain makes more than a Seven-Three captain. A pilot flying to Europe makes more than a domestic pilot, and he's additionally trained, both in navigation and in communication procedures.

To rise in the ranks, you have to submit to more flight training. This is quite rigorous, and there are no guarantees accompanying it. There are many, many pilots who would rather not go through the hassle of it; they'd rather stay where they are and fly a plane that feels comfortable to them.

Pilots like me have an itch for new plane types. After a couple of years, we're ready to move on again. And every time we do, we have to start at the bottom. We surrender our status and have to submit to being students again.

For instance:

When you train for a new plane, you have to begin by going to *ground school.* Usually your ground school is at your company's headquarters. You'll have hours of instruction about the plane you're being trained for, and at least once a day you'll have a written examination on it.

When you've gotten through that, you'll be given two *oral exams.* The first of these exams will be given by your airline company. If you survive that ordeal, you'll be given an FAA oral. Each will last hours and be the equivalent of a postgraduate examination.

When your orals are over, you'll be put in a *simulator.* There, for at least a week, you'll get practical hands-on flight instruction. As you operate the plane, you'll be cross-checked, interrogated. Most airlines' simulators are in round-the-clock use nowadays.

Past the flight-instruction stage, you'll be taken for a *check-ride.* A check-ride is a test. It will be given by a simulator instructor. He'll put you through the paces of a start-to-finish "airline flight," and you'll have to respond with perfection to whatever crazy problems he throws at you.

And, believe me, he can throw you plenty.

When you get through all that, you'll be taken on another check-ride. The earlier ride was the ride your own company gave you. The next ride you take is an FAA check-ride. Each of these check-rides can last three to five hours or longer.

You might think that's enough—but even that hasn't qualified you. When the check-rides are over, you'll be taken for a real airplane trip. You'll spend twenty-six hours with a *senior check pilot,* then you'll do that again with an FAA man sitting next to you.

It's extraordinarily grueling. It's also, of course, necessary. In the history of my career, I've been through it a half-dozen times or more. And every time I've done it, I've had to start at the bottom. Sometimes I've felt as if I've never flown a plane before.

If that were the end, you might not be impressed by it. After all, you might argue, we're being well compensated. A major line captain can make $160,000. That's a nice little reward for going through some training agony.

And that's true.

But consider:

If I were a doctor or lawyer, I'd have one or two exams to pass. Once I'd passed those, I'd have no more to worry about. Even if I erred, I'd have a peer group protecting me. There aren't too many doctors who have ever managed to lose their medical licenses.

As a pilot, however, I am continually at jeopardy. Four times a year—both by my company and by the FAA people—I'll be checked and rechecked, and often without warning. And if I don't perform well, I've just surrendered my transport license.

And I won't get it back, either.

I've sometimes likened flying to being in an operating room. Certainly the skills are analogous to a brain surgeon's. With this crucial difference: You yourself are the patient. And if you don't do it right, there's going to be nobody to cover for you.

By the clock on the wall, it's now an hour before flight time. All airline crew members have a sixty-minute preflight requirement. If you're two minutes late, they'll have to call in a standby. That will not make them happy. You'll be financially penalized for it.

The place I check in is called a *flight operations room.* Depending on the airline, that can be small, or it can be sizable. There'll be some sort of area set aside by your company where you register for duty and review the plans for the flight you're making.

When I first began flying, all such rooms were a social haven. It was the wild 1960s. The sexes were integrated. When the stewardesses came in it was like a Saturday night singles bar. The pilots would stand around and make these not-so-suave comments about them.

Now that's abated. Today, we're more "sensible." Like everything else, it's grown sterile, more automated. When you go to your desk, instead of meeting a flight attendant, there's a very good chance that all you'll meet is a computer terminal.

Wheels within wheels. How can I begin to describe this to you? This business nowadays is so incredibly complicated. People are always saying, "Why do we have all these flight delays?" I say, "Hey, wait a minute . . . I'm delayed as much as you are, mister!"

Two observations:

Since flying causes tension, the average airline passenger tends to exaggerate what's happening to him. A one-hour delay becomes, in his eyes, a four-hour delay. A little bumpy air becomes "extremely turbulent" flying conditions. (To set the record straight on that: You've never been in "extreme turbulence." Nobody has—not and lived to tell about it.)

I had a situation recently in which I got stuck in a takeoff line. We had a

23

businessman on board, and he insisted on getting off again. I tried to point out that we'd be leaving momentarily, but he said he had waited long enough; he wanted me to go back to the gate again.

That posed a problem. I said, "Okay, I'll do that for you. I'll get out of line—only I'm going to give out your seat number. When the other passengers ask why we're turning back again, I'll say, 'Take it up with him. He's decided his time is more precious than yours is.' "

The man thought about this for a couple of seconds, then he decided perhaps he should stay on board after all.

My second observation is that *delays delay everybody*. When a plane is delayed it causes trouble for the airline company. A "push-back/delay" creates havoc with the flight-deck crew. We have to refigure everything from our ice supplies to our fuel consumption.

I can't tell you the times that, unknown to my passengers, I've gotten on the horn and raised a fuss with the ground controllers:

"What's going on!"

"We don't know—they won't tell us, Captain."

We sit. And we sit. And we sit some more. I get furious sometimes.

Usually, of course, the problem is traffic. A controller in Michigan has suddenly got too many planes to handle. He orders a hold, which spreads clear across the country, grounding planes in San Francisco that weren't even heading for the Michigan area.

The traffic nowadays has become truly incredible. Planes have become couriers for our entire economic system. Trillions of dollars rest on every day's flight operations, and when you throw in some storms you've got a giant-sized mess on your hands.

A little later on I'm going to take you through some control centers. You'll meet a peculiar breed of cat who's known vernacularly as a "tin pusher." He's the controller: he pushes planes through the traffic system. It's a very crucial job—and, at times, it's a controversial one.

A friend of mine recently had to fly out to Omaha. The route he was flying meant he had to change planes in Pittsburgh. When he went to cross over from one gate to the other, it was suddenly announced that his plane had some maintenance problems.

"Well, for Chrissake," he muttered. He went over to a passenger agent. "Is there any chance," he said, "that they can bring a new airplane in here?"

"I'm sorry," she told him. "We're going to have to fix this one. It's a landing gear problem, and it will be a couple of hours probably."

A couple of hours. So he went to the men's room. And when he emerged from that room, not three minutes later, there was this plane (not the same as the original plane) and he had exactly two minutes to drag his bags through the gate area.

Now what causes that? Where on earth did that airplane come from? And why in God's name didn't the gate agent know about it? Unraveling such mysteries could take a couple of large volumes, but I'll do what I can at least to illuminate a corner of it.

Each major airline has a scheduling or routing department. They've got hundreds of planes and tens of thousands of route combinations. It takes a room full of people and a bank of computers just to keep the planes sorted in terms of crew times and maintenance service. I've talked with those people. I don't know how they keep up with it, frankly. At an airline like mine there are more than 40,000 "city pairs." That's 40,000 routes that are in constant rotation and have to be endlessly revised because of weather or logistical problems.

When an agent at a desk says that there aren't any planes available, or that a flight's been postponed, or that a delay will take hours possibly, she's reporting, quite faithfully, what she sees on her monitor, and as far as she knows she's imparting the gospel to you. The only problem is, she isn't keyed to the schedulers' monitors. The schedulers' monitors are way the hell out in headquarters somewhere. Headquarters, probably, is clear across the country, and between headquarters and the agent there are who-knows-how-many computer interfaces.

How often has it happened, after they've announced that some flight is canceled, and you're standing there in line, and there's a feeling of dismay in the air, some wise guy behind you says, "They always cancel that one! They see if it's full, and if it's not they just cancel it on you!"

Well, think about that. That wouldn't even make business sense. To pull a plane off line means you'd have to reroute all your other connections. Planes don't just fly to get passengers to airports; they've got to stay in position to meet both passenger and maintenance timetables.

What has more likely happened is that there was some sort of equipment shortage. Another flight somewhere was having an engine or an instrument problem. If the flight with the problem had considerably more passengers on it, the underbooked plane was probably brought in as a substitute for it.

That may not be of much consolation to you as you sit around cooling your heels at the airport, but to the airline it's choosing the lesser of two evils.

Another thing that's frustrating is the communications problem. You push back from the gate, and all of a sudden you've got a delay somewhere. You'd like to get on the horn and tell your passengers what's happening, but you're talking to ground, and they aren't being very helpful to you.

I've often had the feeling that, if our airlines were smarter, they'd employ a couple of psychologists to train people in *communicating*. That wouldn't make things move—it wouldn't solve our delay problems—but it might make some people feel a little less like murdering somebody.

Let's return for a moment to the men up in those ramp towers. There are about ten zillion things that can go wrong on those aprons they're looking at. You've got hundreds of workers and literally millions of hardware pieces. If something fouls up it can rebound on the scheduling department.

Take a look around this tower. Every man's got his workstation. Over there, in the corner, there's a monitor just for *passenger loading*. It's got the names and locations of all the booked passengers, plus their times of arrival, and what flight they'll be departing on.

At a desk next to that, there'll be a computer just for *fuel deliveries*. The fuel for these planes has been banked in huge storage tanks. It's snaked underground to the various gate areas, where it's pumped up by truck and filtered up to the airplane bodies.

You've got another man here, and he just deals with the *baggage* problems. When there's a late arriving flight, he looks up all the connecting flights; he'll transmit a signal to the guys out in baggage and it will trigger an alert to watch out for certain baggage numbers.

Sometimes when I stand here and I watch this activity and the computerized data and all the phone calls and keyboard antics, I'll just lean against the wall and put my hands in my pockets and I'll thank my lucky stars that all I'm doing is *flying* this equipment. Here come the passengers . . . You have to worry about security checkpoints. Their bags are going out . . . they'll be sent to the baggage area . . . and here comes the fuel, it has to be carefully monitored, and you've got cargo to load, and you've got livestock and post office pallets. Wheels within wheels. And what's that? That's a food truck down there. You look through the windows, and you've got a truck—*on a runway, damn it!* Some apprentice is driving, and he didn't see a marker, and he's out there on the runway, and we've got a 747 landing! Gimme a break! And what's this?—we've got weather info. They've got storm cells reported—they've got lightning in Delaware—and there's a guy on to tell us there are a dozen more airplanes coming, and they're all landing here, because it's the only field open to them. Wheels within wheels. It's incredibly machinated. Here's security on the phone. They've got a woman with a target pistol. She says it's okay because she's going to a shooter's convention, and how's she going to shoot if she can't bring her pistol with her? Pistol, indeed . . . And what's this . . . from the ticketing department? (Tell her to take that damn pistol . . .) We've got a call from the ticketing department. They've got a businessman there, and he's got a quick change of schedule, and we're supposed to pick out his bag, which is gray and says "Samsonite" on it.

Lord in heaven, preserve us.

Wheels within wheels. It gives you ulcers just thinking about it. And you go home that night, and you put your feet up on your coffee table, and you pour yourself a drink, and you stare at the missus, and you say, "Damn it, Lorraine, I sure wish I'd took flying lessons!"

At least that's how I imagine it.

Fortunately for me, I don't have to worry about those ramp-tower problems. All I have to do is check in with my computer terminal. The computer keeps beeping and spitting out jibberish at me. Only to me it's not jibberish. To me it's my future talking:

```
1184/10 RLS 2 ATL 1148Z 0648L-TUC 1535 0835L
SHIP 411 H/B767/R EBFT TYPE ECN FL 390 ROUTE A1X
   1452
ATL.J14.VUZ . . . ARG . . . BUM . . . LBF . . . HIA
   . . . GEG . . . PHX . . . TUC.ETE-347 RAMP WT 268200
   LWT 225653 PAYLOAD 137/032000 TAXI 16/05
TARGET GATE ARVL FUEL 12.2 SCHEDULED GATE H05
```

And so on.

Basically, what that's saying is that I'll be leaving from Atlanta. My scheduled departure is at 6:48 A.M. local time. I'll be flying to Tucson, crossing various waypoints. I'll have such and such a weight, and I'll have such and such a fuel consumption.

The computations involved are incredibly complicated. They'll have taken into account all my fuel-burns and wind conditions; they'll have me vectoring around, or going higher, or descending, and it will be figured with a finesse I couldn't possibly have duplicated.

When I first started flying all this stuff was the pilot's job. You figured it yourself—or you gave it to your flight engineer. Whatever you came up with . . . well, that's what you were stuck with. You couldn't have possibly figured it out down to the last fraction of a unit of wind velocity.

Today it's done for you. It's been computed by your support personnel. There are hundreds of people behind each and every airplane flight. There'll be a release form attached that holds the pilot responsible, but it's not just one man, it's a whole corporation up there.

This increased sophistication has led to two distinct consequences. On the positive side, we've made flying so *organized*. We've got routers and dispatchers and supervisors and meteorology departments . . . it's a pretty far cry from guys in flight jackets with white scarves flying. But on the underside of that is a kind of Copernican trade-off. *Homo sapiens* (read *me)* has been shoved from the epicenter. He twirls around the system with a host of gray figures, getting less and less glory—and, on occasion, less money from it.

"Pilot-as-overhead" has become an increasingly big issue nowadays. It's been spurred, in large part, by advances in technology. "Why," ask our executives, "should we pay you so much money when all you're doing up there is reading dials and pushing computer buttons?" We'll talk about that after we've flown a few miles together. I hope to convince you that I'm more than just a button-pusher. A pilot isn't paid for all those hours when nothing is happening up there—he's paid for those seconds when suddenly there's a crisis confronting him.

I've signed my release. I'm going to go out to the airplane now. The plane that I'm flying has just arrived here from Kennedy. I'm going to fly it to Tucson, where it will be refueled and have some cargo changes; then a new crew will take it and fly it up to Seattle later.

As you're sitting beside me, I'll regale you with airline stories. You're going to get a pretty good idea of what goes on in those cockpits up there. But before I do that, I have to make some introductions. I want you to become properly acquainted with one of the world's smartest flying machines.

## Chapter 4

# The Flight Deck

This particular plane is called a 767. It's a twin-engine Boeing. It's one of our more modern "wide-bodies." The model I fly is one of the -300 "stretch" series. It can take 261 passengers and fly them clear to Japan, if necessary.

The thing that makes it special isn't its size, or its load capacity. It's not its power or its speed or its remarkable fuel efficiency. It's that state-of-the-art chamber perched up front, behind the windshield, and which, in function and design, is revolutionizing the airplane industry.

You've been on an airplane—you've probably done this sometime. You've taken a right to go back to your passenger seat. You've stolen a look toward that half-open cockpit, and you've been totally nonplussed by all those gauges and instruments in there. What on earth *are* those? They're like . . . the bumps on a brain hemisphere! There are all these little levers, all these black-matte excrescences. You stand there and stare, and you feel momentarily baffled, and you go back to your seat thinking nobody could ever memorize all of that.

Well, I'll tell you a secret. When a pilot's "promoted"—meaning when he leaves one craft type and goes to train on another one—his initial response is not that different from what yours is: many of those things are nothing short of bewildering to him. On a 747 (I'm using that as an example here; it's an older airplane type, but it's a very well-known one; even as I write it's being completely remodeled so that, in its new configuration, it will have a flight deck like I'm describing)—on a 747, you have a multiplicity of dials in front of you. You've got a console beside you that has navigational aids and trim tabs sticking out of it. You have an overhanging "glare shield" that has radio and autopilot switches, and you have panels on the ceiling that contain a variety of engine cutoffs. It's extraordinarily cluttered. You've got about a thousand different things to monitor. And if you're sitting up front, in either the left or the right operator's seat, you can't even reach around and put your hands on the majority of them; they're mounted to the rear, and you have to have a third man to deal with them.

But now look at my airplane. There's just a pilot's and a copilot's seat. Some 600 functions have been eliminated from the control panels. On the wall to the right, where the engineer was sitting, there's a box with some shelves. Behind that, there's a wardrobe closet. How simple it is! It's not much worse than . . . a sports car dashboard! You've got some computer-terminal screens, and they have some weird-looking graphics on them, but other than that it doesn't seem all that complicated, and you have dreams (foolish dreams!) that you might even be able to fly this bugger.

Let me eulogize its virtues. Not too many years ago I was flying out of Buffalo on a DC-8 turbojet. We were leaving 37,000 feet and climbing to 41,000 . . . when all of a sudden there was this god-awful Klaxon sounding.

I scanned all the gauges. Everything looked normal. That honker going off was our master emergency warning system. But what the hell was it? Everything felt perfect. Was the honker malfunctioning? Was I not reading an instrument properly?

Then, suddenly, it hit me.

"Altitude!" I shouted. I buttoned the mike. I immediately identified myself. "Emergency descent! I need to descend to 10,000 feet," I said, and as I pressed against the yoke there was the sound of the slipstream whistling. . . .

What had happened, I learned, is that we had failed to turn a compressor on. My flight engineer, who had some very significant teamwork problems, had completely neglected this most fundamental checklist item, and the pressure in our cabin had begun to deteriorate on us. In another few minutes we could have all slipped from consciousness. A deficiency of oxygen can result in *hypoxia*. That's a very serious thing, and I had to write the guy up for it. It did not make that day a particularly pleasant one for either of us.

But now look at this airplane. Had a compressor malfunctioned, a light would have come on that would have warned me of my cabin altitude. It would have told me in an instant precisely what was happening, and I could have corrected the problem without the passengers having their lunch trays rattled. Everything about it is so much easier, more automated. It's approaching the point where we can actually hold "dialogues" with it. A few years from now we'll have computerized cockpits which will not only warn us, they're going to flash various solutions at us.

There's a downside, of course. There always is in these trade-offs. In eliminating a man we've also eliminated a creative center. We've stream-lined our cockpit and gotten rid of a payroll entry, but we have two fewer eyes and one less head to help solve problems for us.

*It was an L-1011. It was leaving from San Diego. It had just left the ground and was heading toward the mountains. Suddenly they noticed they had no control over their stabilizers. Those are the parts of the tail that help to regulate the pitch attitude.*

*The plane began climbing. It rose like a space rocket. Had a machine been in charge it would have gone into a tailspin. There was nothing any programmer would have put into a computer that would have helped point the way to keeping that airplane aloft that morning.*

*But what that TriStar crew did was simply apply some creative power. They set the tail engine to run at one power setting; they set the wing engines to run at another power setting, and they brought the plane in using the differential thrust between them.*

*That was a brilliant solution—and it was one based on manpower. In the majority of cases a machine can out-logic you; but every so often you get that oddball exception, and when you do you feel grateful that you had a couple of warm bodies sitting next to you.*

On the 767, we have an incredibly advanced guidance system. It's called the *Inertial Reference System.* It's guided by laser rays. It can sense where you are down to the fraction of a meter, and it can project your whole trip, drawing you a "map" on your computer terminal. This is programmed by a keypad. The keypad sits between the pilots' seats. The device is so ad-vanced, it's been "detuned" by our Defense Department. The reasoning, I hear, is that they're afraid it might be hijacked; it could be used by our enemies to ram bombs down our missile silos.

That windshield up there—that probably strikes you as undersized. There's a reason, of course; it has to do with the light reflection. Flying above the clouds admits a lot of bright sunlight. That can be very disturbing when you're scanning your instrument panel.

The windscreen itself is divided hexadically. It's two inches thick, and it's mounted in liquid. It's got two separate heat grids—one for ice, one for cockpit moisture. It costs thousands of dollars should a bird put his beak through one of them.

Behind and to the right you'll see a switch near where the copilot sits. That's the *"Dead Dog Switch."* There is a very important reason for it. In point of actual fact it's really nothing but a heat switch, but to understand its function you have to know what we'll be encountering up there.

When you're at 40,000 feet you'll find a very hostile world surrounding you. The winds at that height can reach 200 miles an hour. The outside air temperature can dip to minus sixty-seven degrees Fahrenheit—which can get pretty damn cold for any pet stored in the cargo hold. So you reach around behind you and you flick the "Dead Dog Switch." That will heat up the hold to about seventy degrees Fahrenheit. It adds tens of thousands of dollars to every line's annual fuel expenditures, but if your Fido's back there he'll tell you it's worth every penny of it.

There's a device above the console that's called the *"C-Mode" transponder.* That's a receiver-transmitter that responds to a radar signal. It will tell your controller who you are and what your altitude is. As I'll illustrate later, it can also be used in case you're hijacked by someone.

Each commercial aircraft has a specific transponder number. When you fly into an area, the controller may ask you for it. "Ident," he'll say, and you'll press a little button. Your number will appear next to your blip on his radar monitor.

Down there, by your knees, you'll see a *quick-release oxygen mask.* You can go ahead and touch it—it will virtually pop out at you. Unlike a passenger, when you're in charge of a jetliner, you don't have the luxury of waiting around for a mask to drop on you.

To the left, by the captain, is the Seven-Six's *steering handle.* That's a little black crank that controls the direction in which the nose gear is pointed. It's not generally known that, while the copilot has *flight* authorization, nobody but the captain taxis a plane through an airport area.

Look up there on the ceiling—you'll see the infamous *"voice recorder."* There are two different recorders that are used to record flight information. There's one in the tail—that one's used to record flight data—and there's one on this deck: it's got a thirty-minute tape inside it.

There's a hefty little fine if you're caught erasing a voice recorder. You're allowed to clear the tape if there's nothing important on it, but there have been several known instances (one of which I'll talk about later) where pilots have erased recorders so that the authorities couldn't eavesdrop on them.

The point of all this is that you have to be careful what you say up here. Much of what is said is actually said for the voice recorder. You don't want to crash having just discussed your mistress, or the state of your piles, or whether you've cheated on your income taxes.

In a couple of minutes, we're going to be running through some checklist items. We're going to be looking at our controls, and we're going to touch each one manually. As we finger each knob we're going to call out the item, and we're going to say if it's turned on and whether it seems to be working properly. When we verbalize that it's because we're talking to the voice recorder. We're recording our checklist so that posterity can listen to it. You remember what I said about having had to sign a release form earlier? That form holds me liable. It can redound on my family afterward.

The so-called "deep-pockets" principle has been extended to airline pilots. No longer do lawyers just go after the passenger carrier. Today, if they can, they'll hound the pilots' survivors and try to prove to a jury that there was some sort of negligence involved. Nothing is so galling, if you happen to be an airline pilot, than to sit through a trial involving a now-deceased coworker. Not only does his family have to go through bereavement, they have to sit there and wait to see if there are even going to be any death benefits left for them.

Every plane that's flown has its own identification number. It also has a "feel"—even jets have a "heart" inside them. One of the most telling indications of a pilot's experience is when he can feel his plane's "soul" through all the wires and the electronic gimickry. This can prove crucial to the all-around safety quotient. There are still certain things that you can feel before the computer feels them. And when you're seven miles up, traveling at close to the speed of sound, those faint precognitions can give you an edge that can prove vital sometimes.

Other surprises: When you walk into the cockpit, and you go to pull the cover off some panel or stabilizer wheel, there, tucked inside, flashing flesh tones and pubic hair at you, is a woman's pudendum that's been cut from some girlie magazine. *Please,* writes the company (this is in an interoffice memo now; it's a letter to pilots coming down from the executive office), *please, don't paste pictures on the decks or in the trim tab covers. It's considered bad taste, and we're getting complaints from our female pilots.* Well, better those pictures than some of the other graffiti, such as "Come Home to Jesus," and "God Is Your Copilot," not to mention loose scriptures left by born-again Christians who seem intent on reminding you that your Maker is up there somewhere. The pilot community contains a subcult of Jesus freaks. It's not very large, and their presence is phantom-like, but there's been more than one captain who's tried to PA his passengers, saying, "I've done all I can—we're in the hands of the Creator now!"

Speaking of which: When we're talking to passengers, there are certain key phrases pilots learn to steer clear of nowadays. We never tell the public that this flight's about to "terminate." "Final approach" is a term we've found euphemisms for. Of course the use of such phrases might seem bleakly amusing to us—pilots have a tendency to lean toward the macabre sometimes—but it doesn't sit well with some of our executives and shareholders, who have a tendency to get serious when it comes to passengers' knuckles whitening.

These PAs themselves are often open to controversy. I'm very much aware that many pilots are chatterboxes. They're always pointing out that "there's the San Bernardino Freeway down there, and if you look to your right you'll see a McDonald's and two Jack in the Boxes." Myself, I don't do that. What you may not be aware of is that, on the maps pilots use, there are no visible landmarks. All we have to guide us are certain radio and laser inputs, and, if you were to look at our maps, you wouldn't even know what state you were flying over. So what some pilots do is bring Rand McNally roadmaps with them. They like to make the passengers think that they know what they're looking at. Myself, if I'm pressed, I say it's the "Whackamahachee River" basin. Wherever we are, there's got to be a Whackamahachee River somewhere.

A question arises: *But what about the safety factor? Don't all these gimcracks just make for more safety problems?* The reader may wonder if these planes aren't *too* complicated. The simpler it is, the less that can go haywire up there.

I was sitting in a meeting with our chief pilot recently, and he mentioned a statistic which you might find illuminating. It addresses the myth that what is primitive is simple and that those old piston planes were somehow sounder than these turbine aircraft. Back in the early 1960s, when we were still driving prop planes, more than 70 percent of accidents were on account of some mechanical failure. It was not that unusual on, say, an old DC-7, to experience a dozen engine failures in the course of an operating year. Well, now all that's changed. Now we have 70 percent *human* failure. Only the frequency of accidents has dropped toward the negligible. I've experienced fewer engine failures in twenty years of jet travel than I used to experience in just one year of piston flying.

If you were to draw a comparison, it's a little like medicine. We still have our problems—we haven't attained immortality yet—but while cancer is ominous, and we're still felled by heart disease, it's by virtue of the fact that we've eliminated the earlier killers.

Take a look around this cockpit. First, you'll note a *redundancy* factor. That's an aviation concept that's been around for some years now. Basically it means that all the functions have backups. If one appliance goes, it is replaced by another appliance.

Modern technology has increased our redundancy quotient. As we've come to rely more on electronics and computer devices, it's become extremely important that we have backups for backups so that we can keep switching over in the event of an electrical failure.

One of the fundamental rituals that's been passed down for decades and which survives even now in the age of computer chips is a pre-takeoff duty, generally performed by the copilot, who, on airplanes like this, is the junior-most flight-deck officer.

It's called the "walk-around."

What the walk-around means is just what it seems to mean. It means before you take off you go and walk around the airplane body. There are sometimes little problems that are nakedly visible to you—but if you don't spot them now, they won't be so little anymore.

*The weather that day had been surprisingly brutal. Washington National had been closed since before noontime. It had lately reopened, but the snow was still accumulating. It was lying in piles around the wheels and around the ramp facilities.*

*The Air Florida crew had remained sitting in their cockpit. This would be remarked upon later by the NTSB safety report. The door was left open. They were both in their shirtsleeves. There was a blizzard outside, but in here it was Tampa weather.*

*Had they gone out to look, it might have been informative. They might have seen those crystals that had formed on the wing flap surfaces. They might have taken note that, in the previous de-icing, one whole side of the plane had had water but no glycol sprayed on it. But they didn't see that. They just stayed in their cockpit. It was warmer in there. Neither had had much snow experience. They were mostly concerned about meeting their takeoff time, which was now 4 P.M. and which was being pushed by an Eastern arrival.*

*What was about to take place would be recorded on their flight recorders. At exactly 4 P.M. they began to roll down the runway. The first officer was* driving. The captain was supervising. The plane acted sluggish, but the gauges seemed to be overreacting.

"Ah, that isn't right!" (This was the voice of the first officer now.)

"Well . . ." The captain paused. He seemed to be watching the engine gauges.

"Naw, that's not right . . ." The first officer seemed tentative. He was apparently waiting for his superior to say something to him.

The plane lumbered on. It finally rose from the runway. It headed to the north out over the icebound Potomac. It was a 737. It was supposed to go to Tampa. It would not even make it past the Fourteenth Street Bridge abutment.

To the people below, what they saw was incredible. This huge Boeing airplane suddenly thrust through the snow swirls at them. Its nose was pitched up. Its engines were screaming. It was descending toward the bridge —which had bumper-to-bumper traffic on it.

The tail hit the railing. It toppled a derrick truck. Its wings peeled the roofs off some half-dozen motor vehicles. It crashed into the river, breaking apart near the tail section, and taking seventy-three people to their cold, final destiny.

The causes of that accident were both multiple and complicated. The pilots were cited for their inadequate flight-deck training. There were problems at the gate; the de-icing was faulted; there were severe questions raised about some of the mechanics of the wing devices. But the point I'm trying to make is that had those men been more *animated*—had they gotten off their duffs and gone and examined the airplane body—they might have spotted those crystals, and they'd have known the danger of them, and all those poor innocent souls wouldn't have sunk to their deaths that evening.

It's experiences like that, plus the dependability of jet technology—a dependability that has allowed us to look beyond hardware failure—that have led to the formation of some interesting new concepts, such as *Human Factors Studies* and *Cockpit Resource Management*. Simply translated, this means we're looking at *psychology* nowadays. We're looking at the *behavior* which underlies flight performance. And we're basing our training not just simply on aeronautics, but on how human beings *think*— how they actually interact with one another.

In the above-mentioned accident, there were two interesting factors noted: first there was the captain, who kept ignoring the danger signals; then there was his copilot, who was noticing the signals, but who refused to abort the flight even in the face of all the signs confronting him. Like my

Saginaw incident, this was a problem of crew dynamics. The captain was arrogant; the copilot had assertiveness problems. Both traits are deadly in the operation of an aircraft, and the airlines nowadays are trying their best to eradicate them.

I don't say these things in order to frighten or intimidate you. As pilots, we're trained. We've suppressed the emotional factor. A little later on I'll take you up on a training flight, and you'll begin to get a taste of some of the tough, repetitive drills we're put through. But the message I bring is that the job is quite sophisticated; many, many hours are spent in the building of an airline pilot. It's a credit to the system that it can take normal, frail humans and train them to the point that they can keep cool while the Reaper's grinning at them.

We're getting permission to go out to the runway now. They're removing our blocks. This is the sign that our flight clock's ticking. The size of our pay is determined by flight time. That in turn is determined by when we're rolled from the passenger terminal. In another few minutes, we'll be throttling the engines up. We'll have 11,880 feet of runway staring at us. We'll use half that amount in order to get ourselves airborne, lifting off the ground with about one hundred thousand pounds of thrust behind us.

One hundred thousand pounds. Let me draw a comparison for you. When Commander Alan Shepard became our first spaceborne astronaut, the rocket he used—that was the old Mercury Redstone—delivered 78,000 pounds, and we all thought that was fantasyland. Well, we use more than that now to take our children to Disney World. You can *feel* the g-forces. You can *see* the ground blur beneath you. And as you lift from the ground you can't help but note the quiet and the supercharged *swoooosh* with which we're thrust into the stratosphere.

So we're about to take off. We've got clearance from the control tower. The runway before us is eradiating thermal currents. And somewhere out there, out over College Park or East Point maybe, a bird wheels and waits. It's a hawk. Look—you see it, don't you?

## Chapter 5

# The Night of the Hawk

I first met the Hawk when I was in the Air Force in Germany. It was in the early 1960s. I was training to be a tanker pilot. I had just disembarked from a multi-crew practice and was heading across the field to get a beer at the officer's club.

"How'd it go?" shouted Cargill. Cargill was a barracks buddy. He and my pal Jerry Carpenter were about to take the same tanker up. Carpenter, the pilot, was being trained to take the commander's position. Cargill, like me, was being instructed in the copilot's duties.

People sometimes ask me, what does it take to become an airline pilot? What kind of man enjoys living at high altitude? Granted that flying's not as dangerous as it used to be, what are your skills, and how do you differ from, say, military pilots?

It's been my observation that, although flying has become technical, and it's getting harder to tell a pilot from any other kind of businessman, there's something about pilots that makes them remarkably self-confident: it just never seems to occur to them that they might actually not succeed at anything. Myself, as a kid, I was a bit of an adventure-seeker. I was always off exploring or doing something that I shouldn't have been doing. In fact, it was while jumping from an airplane and looking back at the guy flying it that I first got the notion that maybe piloting was the life I wanted.

But toying with fate would not have qualified me for airline duty. Sheer derring-do does not sit well with your employment interviewers. There must also be an awareness that your ability has limits and that if you don't play it safe God will not grant immunity to you.

In those days, of course, we didn't know much about simulator training. What simulators we had were rather crude and unsophisticated. There was a tank, like a cockpit, and it had various arms attached to it, and when you wiggled the stick it more or less reacted like an airplane maneuvering.

I remember an incident which helps to illustrate the simplicity of it. When you trained in a simulator they'd turn the lights out on the windscreen panels. You'd be flying along blind, having maneuvered by instruments, then you'd "descend" to 200 feet, and there would be your "airport" staring at you.

This "airport," so called, was about as sophisticated as the simulator was. It was a little pasteboard model which you were viewing through a magnifying glass. With about five seconds to go you'd drop from the darkness, and there would be this "runway" with these twinkling little approach lights painted on it.

One of our group decided to have a little fun with this. He went and caught a fly and glued its carcass to the "airport" runway. He positioned its corpse so that it was facing the magnifying lens, with its bulbous little eyes and its mean little mandibles showing.

Enter a trainee. He climbs in the simulator. He does everything perfectly as he's flying under instrument conditions. Then suddenly he breaks out into visual conditions—and there's this 50-foot insect about to devour the whole trainer mechanism!

As you can easily appreciate, we did not rely on simulators much. Even the airlines back then did most of their training in real airplanes. It became a grim sort of joke that, although the passengers were safe, the guys in training sure weren't—and that went double for their flight instructors.

At any rate, in Germany we were training at altitude. We'd take the plane up, and we'd go through maneuvers with it. The instructor would drill us—he'd throw various problems at us—then we'd set it back down. And then we'd do all over again.

And again.

And again.

And again.

That particular airbase was on the edge of a commercial center. A train track cut through. It ran out to the perimeter. At the edge of the field, beyond the barracks and the officers' housing, stood a couple of inns—

Germany's equivalent of Hyatt Houses. I had just crossed the track and was walking over toward the officer's club. The night smelled of oil. My uniform was sticking to me. Up ahead, from the club, a jukebox was blaring. "Our Day Will Come." They were playing it over and over again.

Through the years in between, and as I think about this incident—as I remember that song and as I ponder the significance of it—I can't help but feel that it was a kind of a turning point: my entire future life would become colored by the impact of it. We were young and we were confident. We were at the height of our manliness. Like America itself, we had yet to know mortality. The year this was happening was 1963. If there was a place called Vietnam, it had not made much of an impression on us.

Jerry Carpenter, the pilot, who, like me, was a country boy, had spent the last couple of years flying four-engine prop planes. He did not yet feel comfortable in that supercharged atmosphere in which time is compressed and all your acts are in millimeters. That's how jets are. They're refined and they're sensitive. They go like a bat. They have very little play built into them. Driving a jet is like racing on the salt flats. You make one wrong move and the whole thing will flip over on you.

As I paused, looking up, stopping to light up a cigarette (another mark of youth; I had been blessed with immortality, obviously), the first thing I saw was the flash against the windowpanes. There were these windows in the club, and it was like a thousand little flashbulbs popping.

I stood there. I shuddered. I couldn't quite grasp the meaning of it. I turned and looked around. I felt the heat against my eyelids. What had before been a skyline was suddenly an inferno. The night filled with fire. I could actually see the tree limbs shimmering.

The next several minutes are rather vague and chaotic to me. I suspect I just stood there. I remember there were sirens wailing. The next thing I knew I was in the back of a deuce-and-a-half, and we were driving through a wasteland full of wreckage and fire-truck hoses.

By now it had become clear that there had been some sort of air disaster. Exactly what kind was, as yet, not discernible. Some rocket—some missile —some projectile—some *meteorite,* possibly—had landed with a crash, and now there was nothing but carnage everywhere.

The hotels that I mentioned were right across from the landing field. They had been put there for the enjoyment of spouses and dignitaries. There were restaurants nearby, and there were a couple of filling stations. There was also a disco. We had our fair share of camp followers.

"My God!" I said, staring. There were bodies lying everywhere. Whatever had hit, it had rolled right through a hotel lobby. Nearby, in the street, I saw something with sequins on it. It was a woman's spiked shoe. There were the remains of an ankle strapped in it.

What I'm about to say here will strike some as unfashionable. It will strike some as unfit and not in keeping with the times we live in. But as far as I am concerned men and women *aren't* equal; when a woman is hurt it's more dire than when a man gets injured.

The reason I think that is because of my background in the military. When you've been trained to take arms you see a lot of catastrophes. But inevitably they're happening to other soldiers—all *male* soldiers—and you become used to that idea, because that's part of the life you've bought into.

But as I stood there in that wreckage watching the dead bodies multiply, watching the charred lumps of flesh become stockpiled and inventoried, I became sickeningly aware of all those small, fragile corpses and the bracelets on their arms and the little bands around their wedding fingers. There were mothers and their babies. There were girls with burned dresses clinging to them. I remember particularly, there was one, and she had been decapitated. "This isn't right"—that was the phrase that kept offering itself. "This isn't right." I just couldn't accommodate myself to it.

The plane (but *what* plane?—that was still not apparent yet; from the size of the explosion we supposed it was a fighter plane; there was a gunnery range just a couple of miles south from there; they'd send F-4s down there, and there'd be all sorts of rockets strapped to them)—the plane—the *projectile*—was completely obliterated. There were pieces of wing. There was a charred hunk of tail section. It had apparently come down within the perimeter of the airbase, rolled through the fence, and then crashed into the hotel lobby.

*"Over here!"* someone shouted. They were standing near the railroad track. Flashlights were playing along the rails and along the cinder bed. There were pieces of wreckage in the trees and in the power lines. Everything was wet. There were pumpers, and they were dousing everything.

The nose of the plane, which by now had become visible, and which had apparently been torn from what had once been the fuselage, was lying on the track with its snout pointing upward. It looked something like a dolphin, with the ground being the sea it rose from. By following the junk and walking back along the railroad ties, probing with our lights among the weeds and among the detritus, we were able to discern, by dint of sheer volume, that it was a multi-engine jet, probably a bomber or a cargo carrier.

"Here's one back here!"

And now came the ugly part. The cockpit lay bare. It had been peeled, as if by a can opener. Its once-vital contents had been spilled along the roadbed. They lay there like trash. They could have been flung from an express train window.

The first corpse we found wasn't really a corpse exactly. It was black, and it was moist. It was lacking appendages. In the middle of the mass was a flame, like a candle flickering. It was a burning piece of rib. It had a small well of body fat pooled in it.

"Look at this," someone muttered. He was poking with a rifle barrel. There were some air policemen present, plus a number of fire fighters. There were also some guys who, like me, were just onlookers. There were also some guys who kept muttering things in German at us.

On the back of the torso, protected by ashes, looking like a book that had been retrieved from an incinerator, was a black, pod-like object whose contents were salvageable and whose wet, gummy cover still had warm wisps of vapor rising from it.

"Second Lieutenant . . ."

They were poring through the billfold contents. There were photographs, deutsche marks . . . There was a card with a mug shot mounted on it. . . .

". . . Andrew H. Cargill . . ."

I just stood there. I stared at them.

"Anybody know him?"

I felt a new wave of nausea rising.

The next grim discovery was about thirty feet west of there. It was lying on its back with its arms crossed in front of it. There was a small, neat incision in the area of the appendix, but other than that nothing—there was no sign of injury to it.

I paused. I drew closer.

"Ssst . . . Jer?" I said, whispering.

It was my friend, Jerry Carpenter. I could tell by his body outline. He was lying with his head softly propped against a railroad signal. He looked perfectly composed. It was as if he were taking a siesta there.

The next thing that happened has become indelibly imprinted on me. As long as I live, I shall never forget the horror of it. It's not that I'm "haunted," and I don't still have nightmares over it, but it's bound to my core. It's as if it's become part of my genetic structure.

"You all right?" I said, whispering—and I reached to take hold of him. As my hands touched his shoulders there was a crumbling, like cellophane crinkling. I had the peculiar sensation that I was digging into marshmallow. There was a dark, crispy shell, but that was it—there was no muscle structure.

Then—

Deeper than crimson, stickier than olive oil, brilliantly relieved against the char of his facial features, a bright gush of red suddenly spewed from his nostrils and ran down his chin and down the front of his shirt placket. I screamed. I let go. The body fell back again. The head hit the signal. It caused a sickening thudding sound. It was all I could do just to get up and get out of there. I ran toward the road. I had to go and find people somewhere. . . .

For the next several weeks there'd be all sorts of accident investigators. They'd sift through the wreckage. They'd pull out the flight recorders. They'd ask the same questions as are asked at civilian crashes, and they'd piece it together like some dark, jumbled jigsaw puzzle. The airplane in question was a KC-135. That's the military equivalent of a Boeing 707. It's the plane often pictured in those Strangelove-type photos showing midair refueling of high-altitude SAC bombers. The task we were practicing was called a VMC exercise. That means Velocity Minimum Control. It's basic to jet training. What went wrong on this practice was both rare and improbable—but it's grimly instructive of the delicacy of takeoff procedures.

When an airplane leaves the ground, it crosses three crucial takeoff thresholds. The first is *V1*. The *V* is the *Velocity* factor. This is the speed at which you can no longer abort, because to do so would mean that you would run out of runway space.

The second big threshold is called *Velocity R. R* means *Rotation.* That refers to your liftoff motion. When you've exceeded V1 and you're crossing VR you begin to pull back the stick. Now your nose is in an *up* position.

The third and last threshold is called *Velocity 2. V2* is your climb speed. It's determined by safety factors. On a four-engine plane it's the minimum speed at which the plane will still fly in the event of two engine failures.

Our task, as I mentioned, was a Velocity Minimum Control exercise. We'd roar down the runway. We'd be approaching the Velocity thresholds. As we were about to take off, we'd get a flash on our panel indicator. An engine had died. We'd have a quarter of our power missing.

This is no picnic. When you're rolling for takeoff, you often attain speeds of over 160 miles per hour. Should something go wrong, you have to assess it very quickly. You have some 3.2 seconds in which to find the right answer for it.

Assuming your speed has exceeded V1, the only thing to do is to try get the thing airborne somehow. Up to V1, you've been primed to abort. In excess of V1, you have to try to fly it out of there.

If the failure is in an engine, you'll quickly notice a performance drop-off. The wing with the failure will start dipping and dragging on you. To overcome that, you have to push up one aileron, and you have to stomp on the rudder in order to compensate for your power imbalance.

So far so good. But having struggled to get airborne, as you're banking around and coming back for your approach procedure, suddenly your instructor flicks *another* engine shutoff, and a *second* engine blows—and it's on the wing where your first one faltered.

Now you're in dutch. You've got two engines missing. Your whole left side's dead, and the plane's trying to yaw on you. To compensate for that, you push your rudder to starboard. You put one aileron up to try to counteract the rolling motion.

Only there's one little problem: With half your jets missing, and your airspeed decreasing, and your plane going crazy on you, you're likely to find, if you let it get ahead of you, that your rudder is ineffective. It becomes as useless as a barn door hanging out there.

This, it turned out, was what happened to Carpenter. When the second engine failed he somehow busted his airspeed minimum. As his airspeed decreased, he lost control of his airplane. You could hear them on the tape: *"Keep it up. . . . Keep your airspeed up. . . !"*

Fortunately for him, he had that Air Force instructor with him. He had that guy to his right whom he could assume to be infallible. All that was needed was to start up those engines and they'd be right back on track. Piece of cake. *Hell, don't sweat it, Jerry. . . .*

The only trouble is, even instructors get human sometimes. What that flight instructor did would make aviation history. He reached to his left, he pushed up all four engine throttles . . . and the plane did a roll. It fell to earth like a mallard plummeting.

See, the trouble with jets is that they don't work like car engines. You can't push a button and get the things up and running suddenly. It takes five or six seconds before they've got all their power going. It's called *spooling it up.* It's elementary to jet technology.

What that flight instructor did when he pushed all four throttles was to accelerate the side that had both engines running—but the side that was dead didn't react correspondingly. The plane hit the ground and slid right through that hotel lobby.

In the days and weeks following, as I recovered from that nightmare, and as I tried to draw a moral out of the death of my barracks pals, I could hardly eat or sleep. I'd keep remembering that voice recorder. *"Your airspeed's too slow . . . keep it up . . . keep your airspeed up. . . . !"* When sleep did take hold, there was inevitably a dream accompanying it. I'd keep seeing a bird. It seemed to pass like a shadow passing. It was huge and it was fierce. It was out there and circling somewhere. "Our Day Will Come." It became a very real warning to me.

Something you should know about the nature of an airline pilot. A pilot's not afraid—not in the way that a passenger might be. Training has instilled him with a strange kind of hubris. When things go awry, he's more likely to feel angry about it. When you listen to those tapes, you can hear it in the things they're saying. It's not fear you're hearing. What you're hearing is—*hostility,* possibly. What comes through on the tape is the sound of frustration: They're furious that this plane is refusing to act the way it's *supposed* to, damn it!

Have no illusions: When there are snowstorms and hailstorms up there . . . when there's turbulence and darkness and buffeting and lightning flashing . . . the man in the cockpit isn't thinking about his passengers. He's thinking about himself. He's just trying to save his backside up there. *But he isn't feeling terror.* What he is feeling is a betrayal of some sort. He's spent umpteen thousand hours learning to master this tube he's flying. Now, all of a sudden, it decides to go crazy. It dares to disobey! And that's the reason for that oath he expires with.

Anyway, for me that was a kind of a turning point. I became viscerally aware of my frailty, my mortality. From that point on I had a different philosophy: Don't tweak the Hawk—not if you want to live to tell about it.

A good airline pilot has paid his dues to humility. He's very much aware of the dangers he's confronting. If he makes it look easy, it's because he's practiced and practiced it. He knows that, to be safe, he has to have teamwork and stability going for him.

Now you know why, when I pick up a newspaper and I hear about some crash that had a starvation-wage pilot handling it, my face becomes red and I start muttering in my coffee. There is simply no excuse for putting a neophyte in a jetliner cockpit. There are all sorts of businesses that can survive on slim profit margins. They can cheapen their product. They can cut down their labor overhead. But there is no other business in which 3.2 seconds is all that is standing between you and a fatality statistic.

Several weeks later, when I was beginning to recover somewhat, and I was sitting in a bar and getting plastered on Lowenbrau, a buddy, Tom

Tobin, asked me to play a game of pinball with him. I said, "Okay, why not?"

"We'll flip to see who goes first," said Tobin.

I reached in my pocket. I pulled out a deutsche mark. As my hand felt the metal, my fingers began tingling. I threw the thing down and watched it spin along the counter. It was as if by touching its surface I had been kissed by a ghost of some sort.

"What's the matter?" said Tobin.

"I dunno . . ." I stood staring at it. It was the strangest sensation. My hand was still tingling. I couldn't help feeling as if I were walking through a cemetery. The damn thing was cursed. It had the dank of the grave about it.

Then, suddenly, dimly, I remembered where it had come from. When that guy with the rifle had stooped and picked up the billfold, some coins had dropped out. That deutsche mark had been one of them. I had put it in my pocket, and then I had subsequently forgotten about it.

"C'mon, *play*," Tobin prodded.

I gawked. I stood ogling it.

"Aw, hell," he said, muttering, and he picked up the deutsche mark. Before I could stop him, he dropped it in the coin slot. I could hear it as it fell and became engaged in the coin mechanism.

The effect of that act was nothing short of traumatic for me. It was like having to bear witness to the worst kind of sacrilege. That deutsche mark was Andy's—it was all that had remained of him. What was left of his soul was being mashed inside a pinball machine's mandibles!

"You bastard!" I shouted—and I was suddenly all over him. I was literally in a rage. I was pummeling and beating him. It took two or three guys just to grab me and pull me off him.

"Jesus!" cried Tobin.

I was screaming and yammering at him.

So that's how it was. And now, over East Point—over Smyrna, or Anniston, or Decatur, or Marietta, possibly—the Phantom Hawk circles, as it circles each takeoff, just biding his time, hoping that this time I'll blow it somehow. I know who he is. I've spent thousands of hours with him. I don't even sweat—it's as instinctive as breathing to me. But still the Hawk watches. You can see his eyes glimmer. "Our Day Will Come." He's an inveterate optimist, damn him.

## Chapter 6

# The High but Not Necessarily Mighty

The most nonchalant traveler may feel tense during takeoff roll. He'll put down his newspaper. He'll glance out the passenger window. He'll try to hide the fact that he feels slightly apprehensive. He knows it's all right, but those jitters keep rising on him. About 20 percent of accidents seem to happen during the ascent procedure. It's as if the Wrights and their achievement have to be proven all over again. What if we fail? What if somebody's forgotten something? Only the incurably jaded can be totally blasé about it.

The danger of takeoff was shown not long ago when a Northwest MD-80, leaving Detroit's Metro Airport, failed to clear a light pole rising out of a parking lot and cartwheeled to the ground taking 155 people with it. It was the second-worst crash in domestic air history. Only one soul survived—a little badly burned four-year-old. Attention was drawn to the neglect of a checklist and the allegation that the pilots had not confirmed that their flaps were extended.

One thing worth noting: In a disaster like that one there are so many variables that might have altered the outcome. This is not to suggest that the pilots may not have been culpable; but one different factor could have put a happier end on everything. Had their cargo been lighter . . . had the ground air been cooler . . . had it been a different time of year, or had they not had so much fuel on board . . . Just one little adjustment might have made all the difference. They might have cleared that damn pole and *then* corrected their wing flap problem.

I'm reminded of a story passed along by the British. I happened to overhear it during an SST seminar. The designers of that transport, being worried about takeoffs, decided to put in a safeguard to compensate for engine failure. On a Boeing or an Airbus this is not all that critical: If you experience a flameout it will certainly cause yawing problems; but you've still got the ability to fly the plane out of there; by using the rudder you can steer with one engine missing.

On some supersonic transports, this is no longer feasible. The speed is too swift. The jets are too powerful. When an outboard jet fails, the whole plane is uncontrollable. There's no way on earth you can use the rudder to control it properly.

To make up for this, they built in a "safety valve." If you're in an SST and rolling down the runway, should an outboard jet fail there's a cutoff or trigger mechanism; it will instantly shut down your corresponding opposite engine.

Excellent idea. The only thing crazy is that, since apparently those guys had fallen asleep during English class, the name they came up with was a *sympathetic unstop*. The engine doesn't stop, it does a *sympathetic unstop* for you.

God preserve us from aeronautical engineers.

Of course that same jittery traveler who was worried about takeoff and was gripping his seat until the plane became airborne has now settled back and turned away from the window. We're well off the ground, so he's feeling more comfortable now.

Indeed, so he should. I wouldn't want him to be fidgeting back there. But each foot you climb has its own built-in risk factors. Listed below are a number of these risk factors. Each must be conquered before a plane can attain cruising altitude.

# The Noise Pollution Factor

As you're leaving the ground you're having two distinct consequences. You're doing what's right by the passengers you're transporting. You're winging them happily toward vacations and business conferences—but you're annoying the hell out of everybody under you.

Many of our airports are truly disgraceful nowadays. We have airports in this country that are built on old trash deposits. They're shoehorned like parks amid freeways and high-rises, and there's no way to use them without bothering some homeowner. Of course never mind the fact he shouldn't have built his damn ranch style there (he probably did so because the airport created job opportunities); this is America, we're in the well-known "Nimby" (Not in my backyard) Syndrome, and regardless of reason that guy wants those damn airplanes out of there.

To placate these voters, who probably have petitions circulating, and who will turn the next election into a single-issue ballot showdown, the local politicians, knowing on which side their bread is buttered, have devised a neat way to put a muffler on noise pollution.

It's called electronic noise monitors.

These electronic monitors are computer-linked microphones. They're scattered here and there about the airport's perimeter. Every time a plane exceeds a certain set decibel level, a complaint is sent in and the airline is penalized for it.

I have a memo before me that was sent to some pilots recently. It addresses complaints received from Southern California. It's a reminder of the fact that, when you leave certain airports, you have to be extraordinarily careful lest you violate local noise ordinances.

The Orange County Airport, which is south of Los Angeles, and which was parochially rededicated the "John Wayne Airport," is an example of a field that's surrounded by people, few of whom take kindly to having a fairly busy airport next to them. In order for an airline not to lose its departure slots, they have to be extraordinarily careful when they're departing from a field like this. They have to cut back their power, they have to climb at steep deck angles, and they have to keep their flaps down while following precisely planned banking patterns.

The price, should they err, is a denial of slot times. Slots, as you know, are an airline company's life blood. Surrender a slot, and you've just diminished your market share. This is a great bit of leverage, and the communities are merciless with it.

These communities, unfortunately, know nothing about flying. They haven't the vaguest idea that all this compromises passenger safety. You have to increase your deck angle to a point where it can become critical; and you have to cut back your power so that you can diminish your engine decibels.

To see how this works, take some paper, make an airplane out of it. Lift its nose slightly and sail it out the window. Note how it travels without discernible effort. It's built for such flights. It has all the laws of physics going for it.

But now take that plane and throw it up toward the ceiling. Note how it stalls. That's because you've increased your climb angle. The thing will go up, seem to hover uncertainly, then stand on its tail and fall back as if a rock were fastened to it.

The most ideal angle for a plane during takeoff is fifteen degrees—that's its optimal ascent gradient. Do it much steeper and you start to sacrifice lift efficiency. You'll need to boost engine power to keep the damn thing from stalling on you. But there are airports in this country which are oblivious to physics. They want your nose lifted up as much as *twenty-six degrees.* You can do that, of course, if you can goose up your engines— only that's not allowed, because it will exceed approved decibel ratings.

Don't get me wrong: This is usually no problem. We have a buffer of safety, and this is generally "acceptable." But what worries us pilots is that it puts us at the limit. One of these days somebody is going to pay a dear premium for it.

## The Bird Factor

What worries us pilots is that when we're trying to get airborne, and the plane is angled up, and we're verging on stall conditions, something may happen that, by rights, wasn't supposed to happen: an engine may fail—or we may run into a bird migration.

Unfortunately, man isn't the only beast flying up there. Birds, for some reason, seem to think they have priority over us. They go where they wish, they very rarely file flight plans. Every so often they can foul up vacation schedules.

There's a story they tell that, again, has a British origin. A British air company was anxious to test a new windscreen. They decided to do it under "realistic" test conditions: they would go get a bird and shoot it into a windshield panel.

They rolled out an airplane. They set up a howitzer. They sent out a guy to get a bird at the supermarket. They said, "Go get a chicken, and we'll stuff it in this cannon breech." Then they invited some dignitaries to come and be witness to it.

The dignitaries came. They loaded the cannon. They lowered the muzzle and aimed it at the airplane window. The signal was given, and there was an enormous explosion. When the smoke finally cleared, there was nothing left of the airplane window.

The punchline to this (and I have a feeling you know it, don't you?— you've already guessed that the chicken was frozen, haven't you?) points up the fact that, when you're traveling in a jetliner, it's never much fun having anything run into you.

Some models of Learjet have a blade called a "splitter" blade. It's a sharp, angled piece that sits in front of the windscreen panel. Should you happen to hit a bird, this splitter will "fillet" it for you. The birds aren't too thrilled, but it's applauded by Learjet crewmen.

More likely, of course, the bird will land in an air intake. The engines on a jet are extraordinarily powerful. The air is sucked in in an enormously swift intake. It's compressed, burned with fuel, then blown out the back again. When a bird gets sucked in, it plays havoc with the turbine rotors. There have been a number of incidents that have ended quite tragically. Several have involved our new advanced B-1 bomber, which, because it flies so low, is quite vulnerable to bird collision.

## *The Airlines vs. the Forked-Tail Doctor Killers*

Assuming you get up despite bird flocks and noise requirements, and you didn't lose an engine, and you remembered to do your checklist list properly, you're now in a space that's reserved for "general aviation." Among airline pilots, we refer to this as "Indian Country."

The worst Indian Country is in Southern California. The skies in that area are literally infested with "Cherokees." Planes known as "Seminoles" mix it up with "Apaches." Many of them are owned by rich doctors or movie producers.

In 1986, on a warm summer Sunday, flying a single-engine Piper out of Torrance, California, a man and his family flew to 6,200 feet and headed toward a resort to the east of Los Angeles. At the controls of the plane was a retired Kaiser Aluminum executive. His wife and his daughter were also accompanying him. He had a transponder on board, but it did not transmit altitude. The people on the ground had no way of pinpointing him.

Exactly what happened will remain somewhat shrouded. There's evidence to suggest that he may have had a heart attack. Whatever the reason, the plane began straying. It ended up drifting into an approach for Los Angeles.

At that very moment, over a town called Cerritos, an Aeromexico DC-9 was approaching Los Angeles. It had sixty-four passengers and crew members aboard. It was descending normally from a 7,000-foot altitude.

The rest is well known. The planes never saw each other. The top of the Piper hit the DC-9's underbelly. Both planes collided and crashed in Cerritos, killing eighty-two people and devastating a square mile of real estate.

I mention this incident because, in the period that followed, "Something," said the newspapers, "must be done about Indian Country." It was recalled that years earlier there had been a similar accident. That had been in San Diego, and 144 had perished. But it didn't take long for the cry to subside again. The same thing had happened after the earlier episode. There was a cry, there was grief, there were calls for greater flight restrictions, then nothing—just silence. All the Indians sat grinning at us.

There's a group in this country, headquartered in Maryland but with a very hefty membership in Southern California, called the Aircraft Owners and Pilots Association. I'd put it on a level with the National Rifle Association.

AOPA (which its members pronounce "Ay-Oh-Pa") consists of 265,000 small-airplane pilots. When they aren't flying planes, they're writing letters to congressmen. And they do not take too kindly to being bullied by airline people.

What I'm about to say here I will try to put fairly. These folks are not stupid. (In fact, many of them are airline pilots!) But this is a battle. I am totally opposed to them. They are endangering my life, and I can't be philosophical about it.

What AOPA espouses is a concept of "freedom." They think of our skies as being open to everybody. In the spirit of democracy, they think that a 747 carries no more authority than does a Cessna or a Piper Aztec. This is absurd. It is simply not practical. As the driver of a car, you may be "equal" to a bus driver; but that doesn't give you the right to go around endangering bus passengers, and endangering bus passengers is about what AOPA has been championing nowadays.

In the eyes of AOPA, the solution is simple: For a few billion dollars, we can accommodate small-airplane pilots. We can expand all our airports, we can beef up our traffic control, and there will be plenty of room for both small planes and airline companies. In a fashion, that's true. There's been money accumulated. We have billions of dollars in something called the airline user's trust fund. It's been collected from a tax put on all airline tickets, and it's earmarked to go into an enormous modernization program.

The only trouble is, we've got immediate problems up there. Many of those planes don't even have two-way radios on them. They don't have transponders (that means you can't judge their altitude), and when they appear on a screen they're just an unknown flyspeck out there.

This can be deadly. In 1987, we had 1,059 reported "near-misses." That means 1,059 midair incursions which could have ended up fodder for the next morning's headline writers. Of these many incidents, only 50 were between airliners—1,009 involved general aviation. And of that scary number, fully 355 involved private airplane pilots almost colliding with passenger liners.

Let's go back for a moment. Let's go back to those noise requirements. Let's look at these problems within the time-frame they're happening. All of these things are happening soon after takeoff. You have a confluence of crises, and you haven't even reached a cloud layer yet.

In the very same places that have the most antinoise ordinances—New Jersey—Long Island—most of the space around Los Angeles—you're also confronted with the most harrowing "Indian Country." You've got many small planes, and they're literally buzzing the hell out of you.

There was a film I saw recently made by the Federal Aviation Administration. They took a Convair 580 and flew it toward a camera plane. They challenged the viewer: "Tell us when you see it." We sat watching it on television. There was a cloudless, blue screen in front of us.

The average nonpilot took an eternity to spot that airplane coming. He'd take forty or more seconds before he could see that there was traffic converging. That's forty or more seconds within a precise field of vision, and *after* being told that there's an airplane encroaching on him.

A trained airline pilot would take fewer than ten seconds. He knows what to look for—he knows it will be a heat trail somewhere—but that's still ten long seconds that could end up in tragedy. And if that airplane is below you, you may never getting a reading on it.

I can't tell you the angst of taking off from San Diego (which, as I'll illustrate later, is an incredibly bad airport) and having this whaddayacallit —*Thing*—suddenly appear out of nowhere and begin tripling in size every couple of nanoseconds.

"What is *that?*" says your copilot.

You stare in astonishment. It's flying up your nose! You're going to plow into the center of it! You're closing on each other at speeds of over Mach 1, and there's no word of warning from either the Thing or from air traffic control.

The Beechcraft Bonanza, one of our more popular airplanes, and noted primarily for its distinctive "V" tail design, is known among pilots as "The Forked-Tail Doctor Killer." It's known as that because there are so many physicians flying it. These guys, bless their beepers, think they're weekend Von Richthofens. They'll get in a plane. They'll have a nurse or a girlfriend with them. They'll sail around the skies sipping booze from a hip flask and buzzing their homes—or, sometimes, flying to a medical conference. And this is their *right!* They paid a half-million dollars for it! Don't you tell *them* they have to make way for airliners. Nosirreebob! Fella, this is America! They're like motorcycle riders—to hell with all those safety precautions.

In 1988, after interminable foot-dragging, the FAA issued what's called a Notice of Proposed Rule Making. They proposed (and have since ruled) that, within our more congested airspaces, all planes passing through should have an altitude-reporting transponder on them. A minimalist proposal. These transponders aren't expensive. They cost about $2,000. You can get them as rental items. For a rancher or a businessman they're a legitimate tax deduction. When you consider the risk, there doesn't seem to be any real argument against them.

But as of this writing, AOPA is still fighting it. They claim it's unfair. They claim it's a plot against them. They argue (circuitously) that there are so many airplanes up there that knowing where they are will just further confuse the air traffic controllers!

Fortunately for us, this is a battle they're losing. They're like the old cattle barons who have to give way to the sheepherders. But give them their due: they don't give up easily. And with their clout in our Congress, I wouldn't bet any money against them.

# Clear Air Turbulence and "Coffin Corner"

Above 10,000 feet, you start to breathe a bit easier. You're through with the Indians—you're into pressurized-cabin country. On a clear, sunny day you can see what seems to be indefinitely. Now you can relax. After all, what can happen to you?

Well, a couple of things. I was flying from New York once. I was on a

737, and I was headed toward Buffalo. Suddenly—*wham!*—we got hit by an express train. In the first-class section I could hear stewardesses and glassware flying.

The plane began buffeting. My eyeballs were shaking. It was all I could do just to cling to the control column. For a moment it seemed as if we were about to do a nosedive. When we finally touched down, I found we had actually suffered fuselage damage.

What had happened, I learned (I learned this later from Flight Control), was that we had encountered the wake of a 747. The plane had been vectored out of JFK, and through an air traffic control error had violated our air separation. This is one instance of *clear air turbulence*. (Clear air turbulence means there aren't any clouds associated with it.) More often it's caused by barometric or frontal changes. The type I encountered is also known as "jet wash turbulence."

In 1968, near a field north of Moscow, Colonel Yuri A. Gagarin encountered a severe case of "jet wash." Gagarin, you'll recall, was the first orbiting cosmonaut. What happened that day was for many years kept classified.

Gagarin, it seems, was flying with a friend of his. He was returning to base in a MIG-15. The MIG-15 is a very small fighter plane. It was the plane we kept downing during those Korean War dogfight skirmishes.

He was breaking through a cloud. He was at 1,500 feet. Through a tower misreading, he thought he was at 3,500. About half a mile away there was a MIG-21 flying. The MIG-21 is a very heavy rocket fighter.

Gagarin hit the wash. He went into a nosedive. Through the low-lying clouds, he couldn't see the terrain approaching. By the time he broke through, the ground was right there and staring at him. He was two seconds late in initiating eject procedures.

An accident like that doesn't happen too often, fortunately. The wake you're encountering has to be large and it has to be in front of you. Today's larger airplanes are extraordinarily stable—but a Seven-Four's wake can still knock the bejeezus out of you.

A scarier prospect (although, technically, interesting) is a little-known phenomenon called "coffin corner." Coffin corner is a function of physics. There's a true-to-life story that will illustrate the perils of it:

On April 4, 1979, at a little before ten on a clear, moonlit evening, a 727, on its way to Minneapolis, was cruising uneventfully through the air near Flint, Michigan. The captain in charge was one Harvey "Hoot" Gibson. He was a sixteen-year veteran. He was with Trans World Airlines. He was also, like me, a bit of an adventure-seeker. He was a skydiver, a motorcyclist, and a sometime-stunt flyer.

An hour or so earlier, they had left New York City. Their cruising altitude was 39,000 feet. That's about a thousand or so feet below a Seven-Two's maximum. Their airspeed indicator was at around the 235-knot mark.

For some unknown reason (and here I have to waffle; the causes of this incident are to this day debatable; one side maintains that there was a malfunctioning wing slat; the other side says that there was a misjudgment by the flight crew somewhere)—for some obscure reason, the plane began buffeting. It tipped to the right. It went into a barrel roll. With every foot it fell, it began picking up velocity. It fell faster and faster. It began breaking the sound barrier.

What this plane had encountered, and would now try to *dis*encounter, was a little-known phenomenon called "coffin corner." During the course of the flight they had violated their airspeed envelope. The resulting free fall would become famous throughout airline circles.

When an airplane is in flight, it has an upper and a lower speed limit. The mathematics involved are advanced and fairly complicated, but basically its lift is determined by its wing design, plus its angle of attack and the density and speed of air flowing under it. If a plane goes too slow, it will stall and start falling. If it begins to go too fast, it will also start stalling. The higher you fly, the closer these limits get. Finally you reach a point where they practically converge on each other.

This is what happened to that TWA captain. He had found himself locked inside this narrow little envelope. If he slowed, he'd start stalling; if he sped, he'd start stalling. It was a hell of a tough spot. The first bump would destroy his flight stability.

People don't realize just how fragile things are up there. There are four major forces that keep an airliner airborne. There's *thrust* and there's *drag;* there's *lift* and there's your *weight* factor. Your weight is a function of gravity, or g-forces.

In recovering from a fall a plane increases its g-forces. At standstill, let's say, you've got a 100-ton aircraft wrapped around you. But when you're pulling from a dive, your weight will quickly multiply. You may end up in a thousand-ton aircraft—and that will need one hell of a big air cushion to hold it.

As Gibson's plane fell, it became increasingly uncontrollable. Newspapers and magazines began to swirl through the passenger cabin. Things came unglued. There were stewardesses flying everywhere. The oxygen masks dropped. There was a blizzard of air-sickness bags.

Up front, in the cockpit, the flight crew worked feverishly. Their eyeballs were rattling. They couldn't focus on the instrument panel. Even had they seen it, it wouldn't have been of much help to them. The instruments were twirling like a hundred little beanie-propellers.

What could Gibson do? There weren't too many options for him. Training informed him that he needed to increase air resistance. But when you're traveling above Mach 1, the air's going crazy. It's breaking in swirls, and you can't get your control surfaces working.

Gibson lowered the flaps.

A lot of good wing flaps did him.

He pushed out the spoilers.

He might as effectively have stuck his elbows out there.

He pumped on the rudder. He jerked on the ailerons.

Nothing he tried was going to lessen that dive velocity.

Ah, the pleasures of piloting! When all else is failing, and the world is going crazy, and your plane is disintegrating, there's one airplane part that never, never malfunctions: it's that little black box that's recording all the decisions you're making. If by some stroke of fortune you manage to survive this somehow, and you're hauled into court, and you've got a battery of lawyers staring at you, they'll pull out this paper, and it's got all your maneuvers on it, and a dozen armchair experts will start Monday-morning-quarterbacking you. "Now tell me, Captain So-and-So, when you fell past 12,000 and still had five seconds in which to deliberate your future, why in God's name didn't you pull out the whooziwhatsis? What were you, drunk? Didn't your airline company train you properly?"

It's really quite galling.

And this is the fate that awaited that TWA pilot. In the next morning's papers, he'd be lionized as a hero. The day after that they'd be threatening to take his license away from him. Savior and goat. They don't tell you about that in their recruitment literature.

But that would come later. Right now he was plummeting. He was hurtling through space. The plane was still barrel-rolling. At one time they did what is called a "split S." That's where the plane is upside down and swinging out, like a cradle rocking.

When their twirling altimeter passed 10,000 feet, they had fallen 29,000 feet in less than a minute. Their wings were in tatters. Their tail had aluminum hanging from it. Desperately, feverishly, Gibson ran through the options left to him.

"Lower the gear!"

"Lowering gear!" said the flight engineer. (He might logically have asked what the hell good the gear would do them. They were plummeting toward earth like an oversized meteorite. Did this captain really think he was going to pull a smooth landing out of this?) "Lowering gear!" He began lowering the landing gear. There was a sound, like a bomb. It was a terrific explosion. The onrush of air hit the gear like a cyclone. The gear doors bent back and began to tear from the undercarriage.

As they fell past 9,000, now heading toward 8,000, now watching the streetlights and houselights swirl up toward them, they had everything out there but their tongues and their underwear. None of it worked. They kept spiraling downward.

Then, subtly, miraculously, the plane began slowing. That gear hanging down had changed their center of gravity somehow. For a heart-stopping second, they thought they heard both their wings detaching. But as they fell past 5,000, the plane began leveling.

It's hard to understand if you've never been through this (which, of course, few men have; unless perhaps on a flight simulator), but when you're falling like that, and you lose all your bearings, you don't know which end's up, or even which way your nose is pointing. Forget all those gauges—you've just tumbled your gyroscope. The plane's like a drunk. It has some weird inner-ear deficiency. And if you're falling through a cloud, that only complicates the matter. You may think you're flying up, and you'll sail right down a smokestack somewhere.

As the plane leveled off, they were locked in a cloud bank. Where the hell were they? They had no visual reference points. Then, slowly, obscurely, a light hit their windshield. It was a great yellow ball. It seemed to hang like a saucer out there.

Never had the moon looked so good to an airline crew. Its great, golden glow cast a line on the horizon. They leveled their wings and headed straight for the center of it. Forty minutes later they were down, and their hearts were still pounding.

I won't second-guess all the reasons for that mishap. They've never been proven. There were hearings and there were articles written. Criticism was leveled over the erasure of their voice recorder. Boeing contended that there couldn't have been a slat malfunction.

Regardless of that, from the viewpoint of *airplane flying*, what Harvey Gibson did was nothing short of miraculous. He had "Yeagered" a plane with some eighty-odd passengers on it and, somehow or other, they had all lived to tell about it.

## Chapter 7

# Flight of the Banshees

Of course the worst flying problems are very likely to be weather problems. Weather's a ghost; it comes and it goes on you. As much as we know about airplanes and flight configurations, the weather we encounter is often an enigma to us.

My worst weather story happened about fifteen years ago. The schedule had me flying from Milwaukee to Cincinnati. From Greater Cincinnati I'd make a hop down to Lexington, then from there to Miami, where we were due for a maintenance inspection.

"You're gonna hit weather." This from our meteorology department. They had shown me a map. It revealed a classically bad frontal pattern. A low-pressure system was moving east from the Rockies. It was confronting warm air that was coming up from the Gulf region.

The Midwest in April can be a horror show anyway. During the best of these seasons there can be downpours and convectional action. If worse comes to worst, it can roil into twisters. These angry, dark spooks can play havoc throughout the prairie region. But the presence of tornadoes doesn't mean all your flights are canceled. Tornadoes are isolated. They're highly unpredictable. They can pop up one second, and then disappear the next. You try to stay away from them, but you don't cancel flights because of them.

As I started the engines, it was a little before 4 P.M. At that very moment, there was havoc in Kentucky. A string of black swirls was heading northeast toward Louisville. The small town of Brandenburg would suffer an enormous fatality toll.

As my wheels left the ground, Indiana was being buffeted. Madison and Hanover were practically wiped off the landscape. Xenia, in Ohio, northeast of where our plane was heading, would lose 34 people and have 1,600 injuries reported.

As we winged our way south, we had no way of knowing that. Local phone lines were down. There was little or no radio transmission. About all we could do was "put our heads on a swivel" and keep an eagle eye out for what was happening on our weather radar.

These airplane radar screens, which are mounted in control consoles, and which are attached to dish antennae in the nose of the aircraft, paint luminous green outlines which represent weather systems. They are generally more accurate than what your controller on the ground is seeing. The "returns" we were getting were looking more and more ominous. With each radar sweep, the green cloud shapes marched closer to us. In the center of the shapes we could see dark holes, or "doughnut" patterns. These are a sign of heavy precipitation and usually very turbulent flying conditions.

A word or two here about the meaning of "turbulence." Passengers always tell you that they encountered "severe turbulence" up there. Actually, they didn't. What they usually hit was "light turbulence." "Light" is plenty rough, and you don't have to exaggerate it.

Turbulence, among pilots, is usually downplayed. These planes are quite strong. They can fly through about anything. In the story to come, you're about to meet "moderate turbulence." Remember that the next time somebody tells you about the hell they flew through.

One of the things on which I occasionally pride myself is that I am reasonably adept at picking my way among weather systems. I can broken-field run. I go over and under them. I'm like Crazylegs Hirsch, and those storms are the linebackers out there. But on that dismal evening the holes kept proliferating. I'd turn to avoid one, and there would be three more in front of me. The radar looked porous. It was like a bowl full of Cheerios. I banked, and banked back. I started asking for altitude changes.

The rain started hitting in the vicinity of Shelbyville. When I say it was "hitting," let me try to be clear about that. Rain, on a flight deck, doesn't fall, like a water shower. It *hits*. Like a gun. Were you outside, it would drill rain holes through you.

*"Pulling the plug!"*

I was shouting at my first officer. The noise on the roof was making a sound like a Gatling gun. I radioed Center, then went into a nosedive. There was a storm up ahead, and I had to try to get under it somehow.

As the plane leveled off, we were slightly west of Cincinnati. The city itself was in a gray, smoglike doldrum. I could see the Carew Tower. I could see the top of the Union Central Building. It's that skyline made famous by the old "WKRP" sitcom series.

"Jesus Christ," said my copilot.

I looked where his eyes were pointing. To the north, ten miles off, it sat hovering over Hamilton. It was an enormous black cloud. It seemed to reach to the heavens. At a guess, I'd have put it at about the 40,000-foot level.

But it wasn't the cloud that was riveting our attention. As we veered slightly south, starting to edge toward the airport, we could see the proboscis. It was an angry black funnel lowering. It was coming from the cloud and scouring the ground like a serpent writhing.

"Center, this is ——. I got a visual on a tornado," I radioed. "Turn me over to approach. I've got to get this plane down—*immediately,"* and I banked toward the right and began dropping toward the airport. I had seen twisters before, but not that close, and not that angry-looking.

The Cincinnati Airport is actually located in Kentucky. It sits on a hill slightly south of the Ohio. If you're approaching from the north, it can be visually deceptive. You can think you're on line, and you can plow straight into the hill in front of it.

To correct this illusion, they've constructed a light bar there. It's a giant lit cross. It sits in front of a piedmont area. It helps to remind pilots that the terrain is deceptive, so that when you're coming in visually you won't think it's all flatland down there.

"——, clear to land."

That was the voice of the control tower. We lowered our gear and made a dive for the runway. With that twister behind us and that crucifix ahead of us, a case could be made that we had become locked in a biblical allegory.

When we had safely put down and our plane was at the terminal, we all got together and tried to determine what action to take. The sky to the west was like a veritable witch's brew. In another few minutes there was going to be all kinds of trouble hitting.

"We're closing this airport." That from our ground coordinator. If we kept the plane there, there wasn't going to be any protection for it. It was a

DC-9 stretch and cost about $20 million. That was a hell of a lot of equipment to leave sitting around out on a tarmac somewhere.

"We go," I said quickly. I could see the storm closing on us. We gathered our passengers and got clearance from the control tower. As our wheels left the ground, there was a huge wall of black approaching. We got about a hundred feet up—and that's when the lightning started.

On a 5,000-acre campus near Atlantic City, New Jersey, complete with airport and hangars and some of the world's finest test equipment, stands a half-million square feet of steel-and-glass office space; it has a small sign out front that says Federal Aviation Administration Technical Center. When you visit this center, you'll find the Flight Safety Research Branch. That's a branch that collects data on lightning and bad-weather flying. Since 1984, they've been taking instrument-equipped airplanes and flying them into storms so that the gods can hurl thunderbolts at them.

Here's what they've found:

—When you're looking at lightning, what you're seeing is an event that may last one or two seconds or longer. The overall *flash* may contain some 400,000 amperes. That's enough electrical power to keep the state of Arizona running.

—Contained in that flash is both a *stroke* and a *return stroke*. The stroke is from a charge that comes from electrons in the thunderhead. The charge shoots toward earth, gets about ten feet away from it, then a return stroke leaps up and the two strokes exchange energy forces.

—A two-second flash may have twenty-four *bursts* inside it. Each of these bursts may have twenty separate electrical *pulses*. These low-amperage pulses, which last about five one billionths of a second, are what are actually most damaging to modern aircraft's electrical equipment.

These facts are of importance because of the innovations in airplane building. Computerized cockpits may be vulnerable to lightning strike. In fact there's reason to believe that the mere presence of the cockpit may serve to coax lightning to leave the cloud and hit the airplane body.

Of course that DC-9 stretch didn't have many computers on it. Its instruments were analog and it had conventional mechanical systems. But it still wasn't happy about being subjected to hot-seat treatments. Things started blowing, and we had to turn to our backup systems.

This makes a point that I was trying to make earlier: that when you're piloting a plane, you learn to rely on *redundancy*. Every cockpit function has three separate power sources, so that, should something give way, you still have two means of saving yourself. When these systems start blowing, you get a very uneasy feeling up there. The darkness sets in. It gets extremely claustrophobic sometimes. I knew a Vietnam vet—a real hell-on-wheels fighter-jock—who came completely unglued during a routine flight through a line of summer thundershowers.

He put the plane down, walked away from it, and never flew again.

Our own storm by then had begun to curl into a sickle shape. The bottom of the scythe was the part that we were heading toward. The top of the scythe lay behind, in Cincinnati. There was no turning back. There didn't seem to be any way out of this monster.

Weather-related problems account for almost half of all airplane accidents. In the majority of cases, the planes are not airliners. They're small, private planes which aren't equipped for low-visibility flying. Nor are their pilots sufficiently trained to handle Instrument Flight Rules (IFR) conditions. But every so often you get a weather-related airline crash. There'll be a windshear, or a turbulence, or an icing, or a slick-runway accident. There's been one known instance in which lightning downed an airliner. That was a Pan Am 707. Apparently a fuel tank exploded.

The storm we were battling would become one for the history books. It was the most devastating system ever to hit North America. Before it was over, it would strike eleven states and Canada. It would kill 329 people and destroy 2,598 miles of real estate. Most of the damage was the result of tornado activity. One hundred and forty-eight twisters would be spawned by that storm front. Twenty-four thousand families would see their property destroyed, many of them in Xenia, where 50 percent of the town was devastated.

If we could have seen all that carnage, we'd have probably been sickened by it; but right at that moment we couldn't see much of anything. The plane was encapsuled in a sheath of black fury. St. Elmo's fire (a phenomenon of static electricity appearing as long, bluish-green fingers of light) was doing a jig on our engine cowlings.

This is when piloting becomes a questionable career choice. You're driving into rain at about 500 miles an hour. It's pounding on the glass less than two feet from your nostrils, and you can't see a thing because you can't use your windshield wipers. The sound on the roof is enough to drive you crazy. It's as if a thousand screaming furies were trying to scratch through the metal at you. The flash of the lightning keeps destroying your night vision. You have to hold one eye shut so that it will still function after the other has become blinded.

By then, most of our passengers were well beyond airsickness. They were clinging to their seats. They were scared, and justifiably. Everything unbattened had begun to fly around the passenger cabin. The lightning kept hitting. The wings looked like they had halos circling them.

While that was going on, and while our flight deck was buffeting, and while I was clinging to the yoke, which kept kicking and bucking at me, my mind, trying to cope, was beginning to curl and fold in on itself. My sight narrowed in, as if I were flying through a drainage outlet. To the passengers in back, it was a simple case of nausea. In the position they were in, they couldn't see what we were flying through. If they had been up here in front, they'd have been looking around for parachutes. It was like Frankenstein's lab—and we were the victims he was shooting voltage into.

*"Center, this is ————!"* I was shouting through the radio. Somewhere out there, there were an airport and a runway waiting. I had no idea where —all I could see was my instrument readings. But, wherever it was, it was time to get this airplane down there.

Fortunately, about then, there was a clear spot ahead of us. We obtained a quick clearance and made a dive toward the runway. When our wheels touched the ground we were doing about 140 knots. Within seconds of touching we could feel the wall of the storm front hitting us.

Dr. Theodore Fujita of the University of Chicago, a man who knows tornadoes better than just about anyone, had been studying this storm from his office on Ellis Avenue. Meteorologically speaking, it was a day that would live in infamy.

In examining the damage, Fujita couldn't help noticing something. He had photos of trees that had been downed in West Virginia. Only, from the way they had fallen, it didn't look as if a tornado had hit them. It looked as if a monster had come along and put his foot on top of them.

What Fujita was noting would indeed prove significant. It would prove more than significant—it would be a historical turning point. It was the first visual evidence of a phenomenon called "microburst." Within the next couple of years, it would become the scourge of the airline industry.

In a while, I'm going to show you what it's like to hit a microburst. It is one of the most terrifying phenomena you can encounter as an airline pilot. The fact that it was discovered during this same April storm front is ironic indeed, and I've often pondered the coincidence of it.

Of course, for me at that moment, I wasn't interested in microbursts; I had a planeload of passengers, and we had just landed in a disaster area. Within seconds of landing we had felt the force of the windshear. Along the airport's perimeter, all the wind vanes were rotating.

The next several hours are somewhat hazy and chaotic to me. As I remember, that evening was not exactly a pleasant one. Power was out. Windows were shattered. Elevators were stalled, stranding controllers up in the control tower. Some of those hours I spent standing on a tabletop. I had a child in one hand, and a bullhorn in the other. I was barking out orders to some miserable passengers who were huddled on the floor under cushions and Red Cross blankets.

It was well after one before I was able to call headquarters. As far as they knew, we had gone down in a twister somewhere. The entire Ohio Valley was a cauldron of tornadoes. We were one of several scheduled flights that had simply faded off the radar scopes.

You may wonder about now why we fly in bad weather conditions. Why don't we stay put until it's all nice and sunny outside? (Of course, the people who ask that are never the ones stuck in airports. The ones stuck in airports want you to scram, and be quick about it.)

My answer to that is that weather is a judgment call. Flying through storms is not a science, it's an art form. We do what we can to keep the air traffic moving, but if we make a mistake, we'd rather err on the cautious side. At that dismal moment, I had a number of factors weighing on me. I had the misery of my passengers. I had the austerity of the conditions there. I had at least an indication that it was clear to the south of me, and I had the desire of my company to keep the plane on its flying schedule.

After hasty consultation, it was decided we should leave again. Miami, said my headquarters, had unlimited visibility showing. So did Orlando. So did Atlanta. It seemed a pretty good bet that we'd be safe if we flew south from there.

Looking back on it now, it was a very gray decision area. Most of my passengers had been bound for Miami. They were clearly distraught over the hell they had been through, and the scene there in Lexington was like something out of a disaster movie. The airplane itself was scheduled to get back in service again. This was abundantly clear from what I was hearing from headquarters. Yes, I was captain. Yes, I was responsible for it. But I was also a human, and I was responding to other humans.

We loaded and refueled and headed back toward the runway again. The runway, by then, only had about half its power restored. We had enough runway lights to get our plane up and airborne, but if we had had to turn back there wouldn't have been enough lights for landing clearance.

I remember some of those passengers and their expressions as we boarded them. This was the fall of Saigon, and we were the last chopper out of there. They had just spent a night with no food and no water, and wherever we were going, it had to be better than Kentucky was.

We took off about two and headed south for Miami. Visibility was good. I could see the streetlights of Knoxville down there. We deluded ourselves that the storms were well over now. We began to settle back. I even switched off the seat belt sign.

In regard to those signs: I've had passengers who have complained about them. They're resentful of the fact that I continued to keep a seat belt sign lighted. As far as they could see, the air was quite tranquil. That sign kept them pinned. It also kept them from getting the drinks they wanted.

My answer to that is that they just *thought* there was no turbulence out there. They *thought* it was smooth because their pilot was *making* it smooth. There *were* bumps in that air, and, believe me, they were bad bumps. We've had more than one stewardess lose her teeth on a galley counter.

Be that as it may: In a line below Knoxville, on an east-to-west axis between us and Augusta, there was a huge flank of storms that was still doing its dirty work. It contained lightning, precipitation, and all manner of hail activity.

"Oh-oh, watch out."

We were looking at our radar screen.

"Seat belt sign on! Strap in! Ignition on!" I shouted.

As we cinched ourselves in, it was like getting hit by a steamroller. With those thunderstorms around us, we felt like General Custer in Dakota territory.

The hail, when it hit, was about the diameter of golf balls. We quickly changed altitude and tried to get above striking range. Hailstones like that can completely wipe out an engine compressor. There have been cases recorded where they've actually knocked out whole windshield panels.

The buffeting got worse. So did the noise factor. What before had seemed a nuisance was now completely unbearable. The thought crossed my mind that there really was a Hawk out there. It had its talons in our hide and it was determined to claw the daylights out of us.

"——," said Center, "we're getting a possible tornado return."

I acknowledged the message. I clung tighter to the control column.

"The return that we're getting is about five miles ahead of you. It's at approximately 12 o'clock, and you're heading right into it."

Our airspeed right then read about 280 knots. That's a speed that, for us, was our "turbulence penetration speed." Basically, what that means is that it will get you through turbulence, but it isn't so fast that every bounce will become an express train hitting you.

"Tornado, four miles . . ."

They were reading the closures to us. At our present rate of speed, we'd be hitting it in seconds. The only solution was to try to get around it somehow. Only we couldn't get around it. We had too much heavy weather surrounding us.

I've mentioned before that modern jets are quite delicate. They respond to the fingers—they aren't like driving a tractor rig. "Milking the mouse" is how the jet jocks refer to it. Get rough with a jet, and the whole thing will turn over on you.

In the spot we were sitting, we couldn't radically change vector headings. The plane was controllable, but only barely, and we had to keep it that way. If we had lifted a wing, we could have lost our stability. I turned the wheel gently and kept my eyes on that attitude gauge.

"Tornado, three miles . . ."

We just sat there, said nothing. The whole cockpit rattled. We were in a very small world by then. There was us and the Hawk; there was the yoke and that attitude gauge. This had narrowed to a duel. We were literally at war with each other.

It's hard to describe what it's like at such moments. You're suddenly aware of your own insignificance. Like a man lost at sea, you're but a speck in the firmament. Everything around you is so much bigger and so much more powerful than you. I suppose in a movie I'd have seen my whole life passing. I'd have seen my wild youth. I'd have relived that Germany incident. I'd have been blessed with an insight into all my relationships, and I'd have lived out my future a whole lot wiser than my past had been.

But the truth of the matter is, I wasn't seeing much of anything. Life, at that moment, had become distressingly primitive. It was simply a matter of trying to cling to that control column and make the wings stay on line with that artificial horizon in front of me.

"Tornado, two miles . . ."

We braced for the impact. The plane bucked and heaved. There was an enormous explosion in front of us. The clouds opened up in a burst of electricity. It was like an X-ray of God. And we were sailing toward the center of it.

"Tornado, one mile . . ."

*"Chriiist!"* said my copilot.

And again there was an explosion, and the whole world turned white

67

around us. A gust hit the plane, we heard *"it passed your right wing tip!"* and we were suddenly spit *out*—

—and there was a crystal clear sky surrounding us.

Forgive the hyperbole if I say that, in retrospect, I could have sworn that right then I heard a 500-voice chorus singing. It was like a Charlton Heston movie featuring Moses and the Pharisees. The Norman Luboff Choir was shrieking assurances of Deliverance at us.

To our right, down below, we could see the lights of Augusta. We lowered the nose. We asked the tower for landing clearance. We brought that plane down, and we simply parked it and left it there. We were loyal to our company, but there's a limit to everything.

# Chapter 8

# Thirty Seconds over Dallas

What I'm about to say here has its roots in that banshee story. It was fifteen months later. It was a wet, foggy evening. As is so often the case, there was traffic into Kennedy. The visibility was poor, and it was presenting some backup problems.

Flight 66's captain wasn't feeling too good about that. Runway 22L had had reports of some windshear. An L-1011, arriving several minutes earlier, had had to abort and go around. "We had a pretty good shear," they had radioed.

His fears not withstanding, the captain got landing clearance. He still felt uneasy. He made the comment, "This is asinine." Within a couple of minutes, those words would prove prophetic. The plane plunged to earth, taking 112 victims with it.

Let me interject here that, when there's word of an air disaster—when an American or a United or a Continental suffers passenger losses—the news in our industry seems to travel like wildfire. The natives start drumming. It's like an event out in the jungle somewhere.

If it's *your* line involved, the feeling is electric. You can feel your hairs standing. They're like the hairs on an alley cat. You ask, "How did it happen?" You ask, "What kind of airplane was it?" You ask, "Are they going to blame us?" And, above all, you ask, *"Who was driving it?"*

This latter, of course, has an unflattering aspect to it. It's not just a matter of *Did I lose a close working buddy?* It's also a matter of every crash creating career advancements. When you hear of a death (or an early retirement, or someone who failed to pass a medical check), you ask, "What was his seniority number?"

There isn't a crew member alive who isn't aware of this paradox. You feel guilty as hell. You think, What kind of monster am I? But such is the structure of the industry we work for that we advance, if reluctantly, on the backs of the less fortunate.

The crash of that Eastern would create some seniority advancements. The pilot and his crew were all killed by the impact. But it would also lead investigators to look for a scapegoat. "Pilot error," no doubt. After all, who could argue with it?

Fortunately, at Eastern there was a man named Homer Mouden. Homer Mouden back then was Eastern's Manager of Flight Safety. As the questions kept mounting, he felt more and more uneasy. "Pilot error," he felt, didn't account for all the phenomena surrounding this.

Within weeks of the accident Mouden had put through a phone call. He called Ted Fujita at his office in Chicago. Mouden had become aware of Dr. Fujita through a previous accident investigation. Fujita not only knew weather, he knew how weather could affect airplane handling.

In the early 1970s, on an approach into Denver, I had an encounter with a force that I had no explanation for. The plane seemed to plunge. We were almost on the runway when suddenly we fell—it was as if some hand had pulled a rug out from under us. "Whoa!" said my copilot. I jammed up the throttles. Luckily for us, we were well into our flare by then. Just as the power came on, we made contact with the runway. As it happened to work out, we pulled a reasonably good landing out of it.

Since then, several flights have not been terminated so gracefully. There was a 727 that hit the ground in New Orleans. There was an Allegheny jet that fell to earth in Philadelphia. There was a United that suddenly dropped on takeoff and hit a radio antenna.

What they all had in common was a phenomenon called *microburst.* This was the phenomenon that Dr. Fujita had been musing about. It was also the phenomenon that, as Fujita would demonstrate, had been the undoing of that jet that was trying to land out at Kennedy that evening.

At every major airline, usually suspended in training hangars, their entrances reached by means of stairways and catwalk structures, sit giant white capsules—the machines known as "simulators"—which are hunched up on arms that look like the pods on a lunar module. These computer-driven cockpits can cost about $10 to $12 million. Their effectiveness is such that they've become the *sole* means of pilot training. When you get on an airliner, it's a very good bet nowadays that your junior-most pilot will have had nothing other than simulator training.

When a liner goes down, the investigators look for the flight recorders (which aren't black, by the way; they're bright orange, so that you can spot them more easily). They pull out the data and they feed it to these simulators. These flights become incorporated into many of the airlines' pilot training programs.

That JFK crash became a flight on my simulator. We'd fly and refly it. We'd make a run for those runway markers. And every time we did it, we'd do just what that Eastern pilot did. *Even though forewarned, we couldn't keep that damn plane from crashing.*

What we were hitting, of course, was this demon called microburst. Microburst, to us, has become the equivalent of a cancer epidemic. It's a "disease" of our times. We've now had eight major microburst accidents. And unless something is done, we're going to continue to have more of them.

The most talked about crash since the discovery of microbursts happened on August 2, 1985. That's when an L-1011 owned by Delta Air Lines tried to come into Dallas and ended up hitting a water storage tank. The crash of that flight has become the most analyzed in history. The recorders it was carrying were extremely sophisticated. They were reading forty-two parameters, and measuring each to the microsecond. We know everything that happened, and we know exactly what the crew did about it.

What I'd like to do now is fly that ill-fated landing with you. I'd like to take you on a simulator and do it just the way those crewmen did it. You'll see everything that happened, in just the way that it happened to them. The simulator will respond in just the way that their plane responded.

In addition to that, I'm going to read from their voice transcriptions. These are files that are kept by the National Transportation Safety Board. The two things together will form a complete reenactment. The only difference is, you'll be able to walk away from it.

# The Crash of Flight 191

The forecast that evening was anything but ominous. The National Weather Service was predicting a "slight chance" of thunderstorms. There were no "sigmets" issued (that means "significant meteorological conditions"). There was nothing at all to suggest that anything unusual might happen.

The captain of the flight was one Edward N. Connors. He was a thirty-year veteran. He had had over 30,000 hours of flying time. According to authorities, he had a fine reputation. He was what they call "a good stick." He had an unblemished safety record.

The man to his right was First Officer Rudy Price. Price was forty-two. He was a fifteen-year veteran. He had been flying an L-1011 since 1981. He got generally good marks from both his coworkers and his evaluators.

These two men, along with their F/E, Nick Nassick, had taken off earlier from Fort Lauderdale, Florida. They were to stop at DFW, then go on to Los Angeles. They had 152 passengers, plus themselves and 8 flight attendants.

What I want to do here is fly their final approach with you. The majority of the flight had been completely uneventful. In fact, they had joked about that as they began their descent pattern. "Another exciting day in the life," chuckled one of them.

Reading from these comments has a very strange effect on one. The speakers are gone, but their voices live after them. I know of no other calling in which one of the requirements is to mount your own death as a kind of miniature theatrical production. But as you read from these files, you want to shout—you want to warn them somehow. You want to say, "Wait! Don't do that! Turn around! Get the hell out of there!" But there's nothing you can do. No matter how you try to protest, they're going to do the same thing. Their tragedy has become immortalized.

They were vectored for approach. There was a Learjet ahead of them. The plane in front of that was an American 727. The controller asked the American if he was able to see the airport yet. The American's reply was: "As soon as we break out of this rain shower we will."

According to the record, that was at 6:00:38 P.M. The American would land. The Learjet would follow it. Five minutes later, using the very same approach, the Delta would land—only it would not be where the runway was.

When you enter a simulator for an L-1011, you'll find that everything about it looks exactly like an airplane cockpit. The only real difference is that you can't see any daylight out there. The windscreen is black. It's like a television with the picture turned off.

By pushing some buttons, you can bring up an "airport." Depending on your airline, it will show any of the fields you serve. If you want to see O'Hare, you simply push the "O'Hare" button. You'll see the skyline of Chicago, and it will look exactly as a pilot sees it.

When you're flying into "Dallas," you'll see four parallel runways staring at you. Not unlike Atlanta, they're on either side of the passenger terminal. The one we're approaching is called 17L. We're coming in from the north, and it's the one farthest to the left of us.

According to the files, it was now 6:03:00 P.M. A warning horn sounded saying that they had pulled back their engine power. They were traveling at a speed of about 170 knots. They were converging on the localizer beam. They were less than five miles from touchdown now.

As we bring *our* "plane" down, we see the landscape adjust itself. The runway grows closer. We're able to make out the lighting details. The field keeps enlarging just as it would if we were a real airplane landing. We see Hertz and Avis signs. We even see buses and taxicabs parked down there.

Now it's 6:03:03. They get a message from the approach center:

"Delta 191, reduce your speed to 160."

"Be glad to," they say. They've still got that Learjet ahead of them. It's a typical tight schedule, and they have to slow to maintain air separation.

6:03:11:

Now they're locked on the "localizer beam." This is a radio signal that's sent to planes from the runway threshold. Stay on that beam, and you'll stay in line with the runway. This is an instrument landing, and there's still nothing remarkable happening.

6:03:31:

"We're getting some variable winds," says the controller. He remarks that there's a shower to the north of the airfield somewhere. Oh, yeah—they can see it. One of the crewmen even remarks about it. "Stuff is moving in . . ." It looks like they're going to have a few raindrops hitting them.

6:03:58:

The rain begins falling. The captain, as expected, keeps the controller abreast of things. "Delta 191 . . . out here in the rain," he tells the controller—then, typical of Connors: "Feels good," he puts on top of it.

6:04:01:

They're "handed off" to the control tower. Basically what this means is that they're on their own hook now. They're so close to the ground, there are no more instructions for them. They're going to put their wheels down, then they'll be directed to the gate they're scheduled for.

Flaps and gears checked. The American has landed now. The Learjet is landing. Nothing strange is being reported to them. Everything is happening just the way that it's supposed to happen. On the flight engineer's panel, all the lights are twinkling greenly at them.

6:04:18:

"Lightning coming out of that one."

"Where?" says Ed Connors.

"Right ahead of us," Price tells him.

Price is the one flying. Ed Connors is monitoring him. He didn't see the lightning probably because he's looking at the instrument panel.

In the court trials to follow, they would try to make a big deal of this. The lawyers would use it to try to fashion a hangman's noose. "Here were these pilots flying straight into lightning," they'd argue, "and they didn't abort. This is a clear case of negligence, obviously."

Well, if you'll allow me to speak on behalf of those dead men: What Connors was doing was exactly what he was supposed to do. They had seen some convection; that was obviously a worry to them; but there was no indication that they should abort and do a go-around.

A chapter ago, we faced some very harrowing storms together. You could see some of the factors that go into a pilot's decision-making process. He evaluates the data. He relies on his flying experience. He does not make a decision simply on the basis of one visual input.

Connors and Price, who were seconds from touchdown, had every indication that it was a very small storm in front of them. There were two other planes that had just gone in ahead of them. The airwaves were silent. There wasn't so much as a bump reported.

If they had decided not to land, this in itself could have been serious. The decision to abort has its own built-in risk factors. That was a high-traffic area. They were in the middle of the rush hour. Even a routine abort can scare the hell out of those passengers back there.

What Connors was doing—what *I* would have been doing—was mentally computing the dangers of that lightning bolt. He was measuring those dangers against the data from his instruments, and he was concluding, quite logically, that there was no imminent peril confronting them.

The mood of the crew was anything but tense right then. In fact the flight engineer decided to extract some dry humor from it. In what was obviously a jibe at Rudy Price, who was driving, Nick Nassick was laughing and saying: "You get the good legs, don'tcha?"

At 6:05.00 the rain started pounding. One of the crewmen said, "Wash that off a little bit." This was apparently in reference to the windscreen in front of them. He wanted them to wipe it or else rinse it with some rain repellent.

At 6:05:05 they were at a 1,000-foot altitude. Price was still steering. Connors was monitoring him. Connors tells Price that he'll start calling out the numbers to him. Price says "Aw right." They begin to drop toward the runway markers.

In the next thirty seconds all hell would break loose on them. There would be no advance warning. It would just hit like a sledgehammer. And despite their best efforts—all of which were recorded on those flight recorders—the plane would touch ground more than a mile from where they wanted it to.

Picture a hose. It's got a very strong nozzle pressure. You point it to the ground, and you turn on the water faucet. The water comes out and it hits the ground like a bomb exploding. The spray goes all over. It's like an upside-down mushroom spreading.

This, simply put, is the principle of microburst. It's what Fujita had noted in those West Virginia tree pictures. Those could be explained only by a very powerful down draft. Some incredible force had felled those trees like a firehose hitting them.

That such things even existed was considered fantastical. They had never been recorded. There was very little data to go on. In fact, when Fujita first published there were colleagues who had laughed at him. Such intense downward pressure couldn't exist at low altitude, they commented.

The crash of that Eastern made believers out of everyone. At Mouden's suggestion, Fujita had launched his own crash investigation. He had interviewed witnesses, and he had examined the flight-deck data. The conclusion was clear: that plane had been a microburst victim.

Here's what can take place when you encounter a microburst:

First and foremost, you have no advance warning of it. The first thing you'll see is a rise in your airspeed. Your plane will seem to lift, even though you haven't increased your engine power.

So you cut back your power—then you enter a down draft. The draft is so narrow that it may completely elude airport wind meters. This draft, plus the rain, will hit like a mallet. You'll feel yourself drop. You'll get caught in a swirling motion.

The storm's *coup de grace* is at the *back* of the microburst. As you fly through the draft, you'll suddenly feel a quick energy loss. Within less than a second, you'll exit the headwind, and you'll enter a tailwind—and that will rob you of flying power.

Here's what I mean:

At 6:05:12 Flight 191 was at about 900 feet altitude. That's when they were hit by a strong gust of headwind. Their airspeed increased, and they began to go high on their glide slope.

At 6:05:19 there was a warning from Connors. He tells Price, "Watch your speed." He can sense they've got trouble coming. Ahead, through the windscreen, he can see a gray wall approaching. The overhead cloud is choosing right then to open on them.

At 6:05:20 they hear the sound of the rain increasing. It's a veritable flood. They have no visibility. One second later, you get a comment from Connors: "You're gonna lose it all of a sudden"—and after that, "There it is," he comments.

This, in my judgment, is what Connors was thinking then: He knew what would happen, but not the intensity of it. He knew that their climb would soon be followed by a fall-off, and, anticipating that, he was reaching for the engine throttles.

It's been speculated here that they had misjudged that raincloud. Their radar, it's said, may have been pointed slightly under it somehow. That could be true. Radar isn't omniscient. If it's not pointed right, it may show an absolutely clear picture to you.

What *can* be assumed is that they were seconds from touchdown. The runway by then was less than two miles in front of them. Trying to respond properly within a window that narrow would have required superhuman skills—and, in my opinion, would have been impossible probably.

The next thirty seconds are, to say the least, memorable. Even in a simulator, you will not soon forget it. You can feel the cab bucking. You get a violent, sharp rolling motion. Those giant lift-arms are beginning to shake like amusement-park mechanisms.

Amazingly, at first they were able to stay on the glide path. The noise was from hell. There was lightning and thunder hitting. Witnesses on the ground said that it was a solid, dark rainwall out there. Even a few feet away they couldn't see that there was an airplane descending.

The flight deck was buffeting. The roar grew excruciating. Connors was shouting:

*"Push it up! . . . Way up!"* he's screaming.

76

Their angle of attack, which was at 5.3 degrees, goes to 19 degrees. They're sailing in with their nose uptilted.

The plane at that moment weighed 324,800 pounds. It was 178 feet long and had a 155-foot wingspan. Imagine, if you can, trying to ride such a bronco through two gale-force winds traveling in completely opposite directions from each other.

*"Hang on to the * *!"*

That's a cry from Ed Connors now. The engines are screaming. They've got them pushed to the firewall. The plane is still slipping. They can't see the runway. The deck rolls and rocks—

—and that's when, suddenly, their yoke starts vibrating.

Among the various "safeguards" that are built into airplanes, and which are also a part of these sophisticated simulators, are automatic "shakers" which will warn of a stall condition. When your control yoke starts shaking, it means that you're about to lose the lift that's holding you.

*"Whoop, whoop, pull up!"*

That's the Ground Proximity Warning System. It's a computerized voice that actually shouts at the flight-deck crew. Its Cassandra-like wail tells you to pull up, you're descending too fast. When that warning goes off, you have to react instantaneously to it.

On the ground at that moment, the world was going crazy. Motorists were stopping. They couldn't even see the road in front of them. Along Route 114 there was a sixty-mile-an-hour wind gust. Signs were uprooted. There was an overturned fertilizer trailer.

Connors worked feverishly. He was lowering the nose again. If you're fighting a stall, you have to try to get your airspeed back. You push on the yoke. The nose begins lowering. From a thirteen-degree *up* angle, it swings to an eight-degree *down* position.

What's remarkable about this is that they almost pulled a miracle out of it. The majority of pilots would have been splattered across the ground by now. These guys were still flying. More than that, they were *landing* it. Their wheels touched the earth, leaving a six-inch-deep impression behind them.

At the time of that touchdown it was 6:05:52. From the depth of the impression, they had pulled a pretty good landing out of it. One minor glitch: They weren't on the runway. They were still a mile out, and they had Highway 114 in front of them.

When the plane hit the ground, it was doing 169 knots. It rose in the air, touched again, and then flew forward. A westbound Toyota was crossing the highway. A wing struck the car, shearing its roof and spilling fuel all over.

The plane began yawing. It lurched toward the airfield.

There was a cry from a crew member.

There was a shout from a second crew member.

Those white water tanks quickly rose up like specters.

The last voice you hear is the controller's:

"Delta, go around," he's telling them.

Of the 163 people who were sitting on that airplane, 29 survivors managed to scramble to safety somehow; 29 people, sitting in the back of the airplane, unhooked their belts and simply walked through the fire surrounding them.

The men in the cockpit were, of course, not among them. The plane pierced the tank as if it were a bullet piercing an air balloon. Ed Connors and his crewmen were instantaneously pulverized. All that remained were their voices on that voice recorder.

There are several new developments in the war against microbursts. We've learned to deploy more wind meters and use them more sophisticatedly. Some airports now are installing Doppler radar systems. These can scan greater distances and give earlier warnings of wind anomalies.

The best, quickest hope may be *on-board warning systems*. The ground-based systems are, in aggregate, expensive. Given the number of airports and the huge amount of land they cover, it's easier to arm the planes than to try to monitor all that acreage down there.

As of 1990, all our planes will have on-board warning systems. These will begin sounding an alert just as soon as there is a wind anomaly. They'll also provide the pilot with pitch-up guidance in order to take full advantage of the airplane's power and flight dynamics. We might never have had such systems were it not for that Delta accident. It showed, all too clearly, that industry practices were suspect. It was a high price to pay —we lost 134 people out of it—but there's a future generation that will be forever indebted to them.

## Chapter 9

# The Controllers

Between Atlanta and Tucson there are 1,600 miles of airspace. It's not like on the ground—you can't see any guideposts up here—but there are highways in the sky which are designated by radio, and we're receiving our instructions through a series of air traffic control centers.

During my "flight of the banshees," I had an exchange with an air traffic controller. I remember it now, because it seems to be illustrative somehow. Pilots and controllers form an unusual partnership. It's a life-and-death bond, and yet we hardly ever see each other.

The exchange I'm remembering is when we were heading toward Augusta. We were surrounded by black. The doughnuts were everywhere. Up ahead was a cloud that I could see was a killer. I picked up the mike and asked the controller for an altitude change.

"Cleared to 10,000."

"Asking for 8,000."

"Cleared to 8,000."

His alacrity astonished me.

"Captain, " he told me, "you can have any altitude you want. The truth of the matter is, you're the only plane up there right now."

Rarely has a statement ever had so much impact on me. I could *feel* the concern. It was as if he were sitting beside me up there. And, in a way, so he was. He was my lifeline and savior. I was out there in space and there was just the sound of his voice to tether me.

I'm sure you've heard stories about the life of air traffic controllers. According to the media, they're all headed for heart attacks. Their seats are on rollers so that when one of them collapses they can roll him away while they shove in a replacement for him. Well, it is pretty tough. But it's not like Geraldo Rivera tells it. Some of that's the party line of disgruntled union members. Some of it's the invention of a journalistic system in which facts have become subjugated to the need for a story angle.

Our air traffic control system does, indeed, have some problems nowadays. The equipment is old. There aren't nearly enough controllers working. Our radio technology is out of the age of Marconi, and, as I've made note of elsewhere, we don't have enough transponders up there. Nevertheless, it's a remarkable system. We fly 1.5 million passengers every day of the calendar year. Every single minute sees 118 airplanes either in the process of landing or in the process of getting airborne somewhere.

That we can accomplish all that is due, in large part, to air traffic controllers. It's a very tough job—but it's a special breed who's working at it. Controllers aren't "average." If we thought they were average, we pilots wouldn't be willing to sit in a jet and let them guide us anywhere.

In 1981, after the infamous controllers' strike, we faced a genuine crisis in our air traffic control system. We lost 11,500 highly skilled workers, and we had to fill in the gap with supervisors and inexperienced people. It was a bitter situation. The memories still rankle. In the eight years since then, they've put a whole different workforce in there. The suggestion that the government should rehire the old PATCO workers does not sit too well with some of the newer, more youthful controllers.

Part of the problem is in the controller's personality. Controllers, by nature, are fiercely independent. They're extremely territorial. They have above-average intelligence, and they have a renegade streak that stoutly demands to see that "justice" is meted out. On a scale of cantankerousness, I'd say they rival us airline pilots. Ask them their opinion, they'll come down like an anvil on you. There's been more than one journalist who's asked a question of some controllers, only to watch them square off and start to shout and disagree with each other.

What makes a good controller is, at best, a conundrum. What he is *not*, say the experts, is cautious or contemplative. If you were to ask your accountant to shove planes across a radar console, he'd plot it all out—and they'd all end up in a junk heap somewhere.

An air traffic controller is analogous to a quarterback. He's a Montana, a Simms. He can think while the play is in motion. He decides, redecides, keeps a half-dozen options open, and he never gets ruffled no matter how many obstacles confront him.

The best air controllers are in our busiest air corridors. A little later on I'll pay homage to the Chicago people. The O'Hare guys are tops. They've had their share of bad publicity lately, but when you're flying through ORD you're playing in a very big league traffic circuit.

There's also top talent in New York and Los Angeles. For the purposes of this chapter I'm going to be talking about the New York corridor. What makes New York tough is that there are so many airports surrounding it. There are about thirty different fields, with a half dozen of them being major ones.

At a small suburban airport out in Islip, Long Island, about fifty miles east of both Kennedy and La Guardia, stands a low, red brick building that has the FAA logo on it. This is what controllers call "the center"—meaning the New York Control Center.

The New York Center is an *"en route" air center.* There are twenty-three such centers serving all U.S. airspace. In addition to those, there are approach centers and terminal towers. They all work in concert. They're like a team working a zonal strategy.

When you enter this center, you'll see a room full of radar consoles. Each of these consoles has a porthole-shaped screen on top of it. There are twenty-eight screens handling twenty-eight air sectors. There are also numerous consoles handling a variety of other activities.

When you look at a screen, you'll see the Greater New York coastal area. It will show Long Island on the right, and you'll see New Jersey and the Connecticut shoreline. On the left of the screen you'll see eastern Pennsylvania. You can illuminate each area by pushing buttons on the control panel.

This picture is gerrymandered into a number of "air sectors." Each of these sectors has a controller in charge of it. Every group of controllers is being watched by a supervisor. The supervisors, in turn, are responsible to area managers.

When an airplane arrives—let's say it's coming in from Italy this time—it will appear as a blip; it will look like a star out there. At any given time there may be hundreds of stars in motion. Each controlled blip will have pieces of information appended to it.

When the plane first appears, it will be coming from the ocean. It will be entering the system above 18,000 feet. It will progress, following instructions, through the various air sectors. It will turn and descend according to the instructions that are radioed to it.

Eventually it will be lowered to about 11,000 feet. At this point, the plane will be in the vicinity of the airport. The New York Center will then "hand off" the aircraft, and the pilot will switch frequencies and start listening to the *approach controller.*

If you're a controller in New York (which puts you at the GS-14 level; that's about as high as you can go on the Civil Service pay scale; the less skillful workers work in less busy air corridors; the pay may be less, but then there are fewer cost-of-living headaches)—if you're one of these controllers, chances are you're quite youthful. Once you're past thirty, you've exceeded the FAA's hiring age. The burnout starts hitting at about thirty-five to forty. There may be controllers who are older, but not many, and not in the New York area.

It seems to be a profession for people who "can't find themselves." There are controllers with doctorates. There are others who are of drop-out caliber. What they seem to have in common is the ability to think visually. When they aren't moving planes, they're on a break playing (you guessed it) video games.

A topflight controller can make about $60,000. He has to be willing to submit to the most rigorous work schedules. There are planes in the air every day, every minute. He'll work eight-hour shifts, and he'll be required to work overtime sometimes.

About one out of five controllers is not a "he"—there are women controllers. They, like the men, have to be able to think visually. Back in World War II most of our controllers were female. It's only since 1981 that they've started to fill up the ranks again.

Journalists and controllers have a hard time communicating. Journalists ask questions that the controllers think are asinine. They'll ask, "What is it like to look at all those little radar blips and know that each is a plane that has hundreds of innocent people on it?" The controller will just stand there. His eyes will glaze over. He'll say, "Hell, those aren't planes—those are just blips on a radar, dummy!" and he'll turn and walk away, and he'll think, "Christ, what an idiot! If I thought those were *planes* they'd have to throw me in a nuthatch somewhere!"

This is not that dissimilar to what I encounter as an airline pilot. People in the media are always applying the wrong emotions to me. People who view life in terms of fear and high drama have no business piloting—and no business being controllers either.

Even at this center, there are stars and there are superstars. Every bank of monitors has a person who is supervising it. When things get exciting and a sector starts jamming, they'll send in a substitute who's like the reliefer in a baseball bullpen.

"Help Jack," says the super—and the reliefer takes Jack's place. In front of him is a screen that's about to snarl in a logjam. There are seventeen planes headed straight for a collision, and he has about ninety-five seconds in which to get all their vectors sorted.

But hey, man, no problem. He starts rattling commands at them. He'll tell two to turn left. He'll tell three to reduce airspeed. He'll tell this guy to climb, he'll tell that guy to drop a bit, and the pilots will respond with rarely a question as to the reason for it.

While that's going on, and while you're standing there gawking at him, and while there are about 5,000 lives that seem to be hanging in the balance up there, this iceman . . . this sphinx . . . this guy who's sitting with his feet on his desk, will be talking to a friend about what happened on a fishing trip yesterday. Doesn't bother him. Hell, he's cool as a cucumber. He's like those guys in the majors who they bring in in World Series games. Show him the plate—he'll just burn in the fast ball. It's like a game of Pac Man Junior, only with a life-or-death ante riding on it.

The object of this exercise is to try to keep all those airplanes separated. At any given time, there may be 600 planes to follow. At a center like this, you have to maintain five miles of air separation. If you violate that, you'll have some interesting things come down on you.

Below each control room, in a room that's kept dustfree—the bailiwick of technicians and various underpraised maintenance people—there are rows of computers that back up these radar monitors and whose continuous well-being is crucial to our traffic system. One of these computers is an IBM mainframe. It has lead-ins connected to the various radarscopes. When there's an airspace violation it's recorded on this mainframe; a warning goes off and is sent back upstairs to the area manager's console.

This is the "Snitch." It's the bane of all traffic controllers. Obviously its purpose is to save lives and keep things honest up there. But from the controller's point of view it has the mind of a computer. And computers, as we know, can be among our least intelligent working partners.

Let's say it's a Friday. Say the traffic's really building on you. You're staring at your screen, and you've got all these little blips in front of you. You know from experience that if you move them all such-and-such a way, they'll be perfectly all right; they'll have the legitimate amount of space between them. The only trouble is, there may be something unexpected happening. A Lufthansa, let's say, decides to lay off his airspeed slightly.

83

The Iberia behind him, who's in a descent configuration, passes four point nine miles behind the Lufthansa's tail section.

Well, for God's sake! you think. I mean, gimme a break, fellas! Four point nine miles! That's hardly a catastrophe, is it? Nevertheless, the Snitch begins beeping. You'll spend the next twenty minutes having to account to various overseers.

When a beeper goes off, the controllers have a name for this. They call it a "deal." Deals are talked of disparagingly. Too many deals, and you'll have all kinds of hell to pay. The hell may be *just,* but that won't make it any easier for you.

There are two kinds of deals. There are controlled deals and *un*controlled deals. The ones that are controlled are like the Lufthansa and the Iberia incident. You knew what you were doing, it was just a "technical" violation. Nobody's going to scold you because some pilot did something unexpected up there.

An *un*controlled deal is an entirely different story. An uncontrolled deal means that, in some way, you blew it. You may have had reason—there may have been too many craft to follow—but it was still a mistake, and now there will have to be an inquiry initiated.

An uncontrolled deal will lead to what controllers call a "look back." Your record will be examined to see if you have a history of "deal-making." If this was your first, they'll let it go as a freebie. If it was your second or third, that will lead to yet further inquiry.

There's a misunderstanding, perpetuated by media and promulgated by workers who see a chance to gain sympathy out of it, that a controller who errs is banished to purgatory. He's slung on a rack and has hot, bubbling acid poured on him. That's not quite true. What he's given is brush-up training. After all, this is government. You don't just go and fire government people. Good Uncle Sam has an infinity of patience. If a controller can't hack it, he's just transferred to the boondocks somewhere.

There are a few basic sins that can lead to genuine deal trouble. One is the discovery that your deal was intentional. Another is the discovery that you were guilty of negligence—instead of doing your job, you were off talking to your buddies somewhere.

There is one Cardinal Sin that is considered unatonable. Your union can't help you, and neither can the government help you. If you've committed a deal and you've *failed to report it,* you can pack up your bags— you're on the next Greyhound out of there.

There's a well-known story that happened ten or twelve years ago. A Soviet Aeroflot was flying into Kennedy. A local controller had a beef against the Russians. He conveniently "forgot" and erased the plane's data from the computer system. For a number of minutes, they had this unexplained aircraft up there. What the hell was it? And what the hell was its altitude? Had that Aeroflot crashed, there would have been an international brouhaha. Fortunately, it didn't—and that controller was soon out of there.

The New York Center is, by far, the world's largest. It handles up to 6,000 planes during each and every workday. Many of these planes are in the process of descending. As they near their destination, they're handed off to the _approach control center._

The approach control center is in a community called Westbury. It's just slightly to the east of both La Guardia and Kennedy. Like the controllers at Islip, these are at the highest GS level. To have worked New York's approach is a plum on one's job resumé.

The lighting at this center is about as dim as in a gambling casino. The room is pitch dark. There are these eerie green monitors glowing. It takes about ten or twelve minutes for your eyes to get accustomed to it. It's all you can do to keep from asking where the crap tables are located.

The Greater New York area is literally infested with airports. Three of them are huge. They are among the world's busiest. Kennedy and La Guardia, plus Newark in New Jersey, have about 3,100 planes either arriving or departing daily from them.

In addition to these, there is also Philadelphia. There's Morristown, New Jersey, Islip-MacArthur Airport, Stewart Air Force Base, and Westchester Airport. There's one airport, Teterboro, which, in general aviation, handles about as many planes a day as the facility at Kennedy does.

What the approach center is handling is an incredibly dense traffic pattern. The planes out at Islip had five miles of space between them. Here, nearer touchdown, they're pared down to three miles. Three miles of airspace doesn't allow you much elbow room.

There are stories they tell about some guys who have tried to make it here. They'll have some hotshot young guy who thinks he knows about air traffic control. He'll say, "Give me a try—I can handle this console," and he'll pull up a chair and start to sort out the traffic patterns. I was given a statistic that will give you an idea of it: Within a ten-mile radius of the Statue of Liberty, at any given moment there may be 300 airplanes circling. Nor will they be cruising—they will be in some sort of altitude transition.

This guy will just freeze. "Holy mackerel," he'll mutter. Three miles of space begins to look like three centimeters. After ten or fifteen minutes he'll get up and walk out again. That's the Big Apple for you. Frank Sinatra sings songs about that.

As I said, there's a bonding between pilots and air traffic controllers. It's a bond built on trust. It gets to be almost religious sometimes. Pilots and controllers have an enormous amount of faith in one another. It's like the bond that exists between the trapeze flyer and the trapeze catcher. Our radio chatter is polite and perfunctory. We don't use bad words. We don't engage in witticisms. Radio space is our most precious commodity. The pilot who abuses it can say good-bye to his pilot's license.

There's an anecdote I heard that supposedly happened in Chicago. It was a Friday night rush, and the congestion was incredible. The controller at O'Hare was like a tobacco auctioneer. He was reeling off vectors and giving speed changes and altitude changes.

"Aw, hell," said one of the pilots, "now I'm all fucked up up here."

There was a moment of silence.

*"Who said that?"* cried the controller.

There was another long silence. There was nothing but static crackling. Then, barely audible:

"I'm fucked up, but not *that* fucked up."

I myself have had incidents where a controller has saved it for me. The skies have been crowded. There have been snowstorms or thunderstorms coming. I'll have been flying all night, and I'll be feeling the toll from it. The controller, sympathetic, will try to lighten the burden for me. Once safely landed, I'll place a call to the control center. "Do me a favor. This is ———," I'll tell them. "Tell that controller I appreciate what he did for me. That was real tough up there, and he made it a hell of a lot easier for me."

Similarly, there will be pilots who will call to apologize sometimes. They will have questioned a judgment. They'll have missed an instruction given. Once safely down, they'll place a call to the control center: "Sorry," they'll say, "I guess it got a little hairy up there."

This raises a point often missed by the public: The impression is given that it's *planes* that cause air congestion. That's not quite right. The real problem is *radio* congestion. We're flying near Mach 1 while using old-fashioned voice communication.

If you were to sit on a flight deck and put on a headset and listen to what's happening on an approach to La Guardia, you would be absolutely astounded at the number of instructions given. It never shuts up. It's like an overcrowded party line. The problem for us is that we're always getting "stepped on." We start to say something, and there's some guy ahead of us.

In the blizzard of voices, it's easy to make errors. Headings and altitudes begin to blur into flight identification numbers.

There are plans in the works that will correct this deficiency. There's a new kind of system which the experts call "Datalink." This is a computerized system which works by transponder. It will communicate visual data directly to your flight-deck console. I'll be talking about that when we're talking about what the future holds. This is all part and parcel of a multi-billion-dollar improvement program. Unfortunately, for now it's only a plan on the drawing boards, and until it gets off we're going to be confronted with radio congestion.

Flying international presents another set of circumstances. By worldwide consent, all controllers speak English. The only trouble is, many of them don't speak such good English. And often the pilots aren't much better than the controllers they're talking to.

*Captain Jacob Louis Veldhuyzen van Zanten was an exemplary pilot. At fifty years of age, he had more than 11,000 hours flying time. The people he worked for at KLM Airlines had such confidence in him that they had made him head of their training department.*

*On this particular day, Captain Van Zanten felt frazzled. They had been detoured from Las Palmas because of a terrorist bomb incident. As their 747 sat on the runway at Tenerife, he began stroking the throttles in anticipation of takeoff clearance.*

*His copilot, Klass Meurs, asked for clearance from the control tower. The voice of the controller was thick, Spanish-accented. "We go," said Van Zanten, and he began pushing the throttles. In his failure to understand, he thought that he had been given a takeoff clearance.*

*Further down the runway there was another big jumbo lumbering. This, too, was a Boeing. It had gotten lost in a ground fog out there. It was a Pan Am Clipper, and it was groping for an exit ramp. It heard the Spanish controller, and it heard the Dutch pilot's reply to him.*

*The KLM copilot said, "We are now—eh—taking off."*

*What the control tower heard was: "We are now AT takeoff." Pretty strange English, but then the controller was Spanish. He assumed that what they were saying was that they were standing at takeoff position.*

*"Okay—" said the controller, and he was about to say "stand by" when the Pan Am first officer got on to make their presence known. The "stand by" got canceled amid the Pan Am's remonstrance, and all the KLM crew heard was "Okay—" and then there was a frequency jam-up.*

*The collision that followed killed 583 people. The KLM hit the Pan Am and exploded like an incendiary bomb. Interestingly, Van Zanten's final words were in English. They were clear as a bell.*

*"Oh, shit," he told the voice recorder.*

Keep moving with the traffic. Those planes haven't landed yet. Approach will take them down to about the 2,000-foot level. From there they'll be handed to the controller at the airport. He'll bring them on down, then turn them over to the *ground controller.*

The tower at Kennedy, which sits in front of the International Arrivals Building, and which is eleven stories tall, including the control booth on top of it, has seven workstations that look out across the airport. At any given time there will be six to a dozen controllers standing around them.

Some of these stations handle landings and departures. There are three major runways. One of them is a "super" runway. It runs 14,572 feet, and is an alternative strip for bringing down the space shuttle. Other tower stations will be designated "ground control." Ground control handles all the traffic on the taxiways. This particular field is one of America's busiest. Those taxiways down there can get like supermarket loading areas.

The security of these facilities is, of course, always paramount. Should a control center fail, the results could be disastrous. I, myself, as a pilot, had a firsthand experience with this. I was a first officer at the time, and I was flying an international route.

We were descending toward Caracas when the tower had a terrorist threat.

"Control, this is ——."

I kept trying to identify myself.

"Stand by," said the tower—and then there was silence. And then crackling noises.

"Center, this is——!"

All I could hear was blank static out there.

After a futile half-hour, we became increasingly desperate. We had 200 passengers, and we were running out of fuel reserves. If it wasn't for my captain remembering an obscure alternate landing site, we could have been sitting in the drink while Venezuela got its politics straightened out.

The facilities at Kennedy have a number of security contingencies. There are emergency plans for evacuating the control tower. Portable facilities can be deployed around the airport so that the controllers can keep working and the traffic will keep moving properly.

They've occasionally had problems. There was the time they had a tower fire. Some wiring gave way and they had flames in a control console.

In a room full of smoke, the controllers kept working. Firemen, wearing slickers, opened holes through the roof ventilator.

There was the time, equally fabled, in which they were the victims of a bomb threat. It was decided by management that the controllers shouldn't know about it. The control room was sealed. There were sniff dogs and bomb experts. When a controller went to the john, he found himself being frisked by FBI agents.

That notwithstanding, it seems to be a reasonably secure work environment. This has long been a subject that we pilots have been concerned about. Should something take place that contaminates our control network, the entire Western world would come grinding to a standstill.

A few things you'll learn if you start hanging around control centers:

1. A thunderstorm—anywhere—plays havoc with the control system. Not only does it affect planes that are headed toward the storm front, but, since these have to be vectored, they will in turn clog up other route systems.

2. A controller hasn't the time to explain the reason for flight delays. He himself may not know. It may be an event across the country somewhere. But even if he knows, he can't always communicate it. There are too many pilots, and there would be too much repetition involved.

3. We can thank good controllers for the fact that we aren't more delayed. The slightest hesitation adds to the space between our airplanes out there. Like the merge on a freeway, the congestion keeps building. If you're the hundredth plane back, you're going to have a good long wait ahead of you.

There's a saying among controllers: "An air traffic controller adds a mile of separation for every kid and every near miss he's had." That's why controllers tend to retire in their forties. Where they go, I'm not sure. I just know they take my blessings with them.

# Chapter 10

# The Passengers

There are three major cities that might be called our "Excedrin Capitals." They are New York, Miami, and Montreal, Canada. Why this is so I'd be reluctant to theorize, but when you fly through those towns you always encounter a passenger problem.

I remember an incident when I was still a first officer. We were leaving Montreal, and we were flying to Miami. We had just leveled off over the St. Lawrence River when a phone call came up, and it was from one of the flight attendants.

Now we guys who are pilots haven't been trained to be psychiatrists. That's probably too bad—it would be a very handy skill to have. It certainly is true that we have to deal with many people, and if we don't do it right it can have very serious consequences for us. But the fact of the matter is, we have no formal "people skills." We get by on our wits and however God endowed us. The things that we've learned we've either learned in the military or else picked up, at random, in the course of many flying hours.

On this particular occasion, the culprit was female. She was a French Canadian, and she was smoking in the no-smoking section. When the phone call came up, the captain responded to it. He said, "You fly the plane. I'll go back and try to reason with her."

Let me say at this point that, in the nightclubs and cocktail lounges, on the ski slopes and golf links where airline folk congregate, it's generally acknowledged that, since we've had lower airfares, the caliber of passengers has notably deteriorated. The horrors are legion. I was flying in my civvies once. They had a druggie on board, and he was whacked out on silly powder. I spent most of the flight keeping him pinned to his seat cushion so that he couldn't run amok and tear the clothes off a flight attendant.

I had another case once in which the guy brought a suit against me. Never mind the fact that he was drunk and he was slugging people. When I tried to intervene, he tried to claim that I was assaulting him. I spent the next several months sitting on the phone with our legal department.

So it's a pretty far cry from what we had back in the regulation period. Back then, well-heeled passengers wore ties and had their shoes shined properly. What we get on board now may be ill-mannered street people whose dress and behavior can be pretty obnoxious sometimes.

This particular Canadian did not resemble a "street person." She wore a luxurious fur coat and seemed to be fashionable and high-bred. But when the captain went back and asked her to put out her cigarette, she began cursing and screaming—and then she began swinging at him.

Of course the worst airline passengers are often guys who have pilot's licenses. Being an amateur pilot doesn't equip you for airline duty. The world of big jets is not the same as the Piper world. The skills are all different, and so are the rules we fly by. Nevertheless, we get these guys with their solo licenses. They've got a hundred hours flying and a case full of airport maps. They promptly sound off, telling everyone around them that the jets aren't in sync or that that's an illegal right turn we're making.

They drive us nuts.

But we also get people who are rude and belligerent. We get people whose fear leads to rage and wild temper tantrums. We get the nicest kind of people who, on land, might be saintly, but who, once in the air, exhibit fangs and have talons showing.

"Now hold on," said the captain as she drew back to hit him (you'll remember we left them just as the woman was swinging at him)—"hold on and calm down. I want you to stop a minute and think about it. I want to explain a few things about the nature of airline travel."

And he did. It went something like this:

"As captain," he said, "I am responsible for this airplane. Assaulting me is a federal offense. Should you persist in screaming and trying to attack me, you will be in flagrant violation of half a dozen FAA statutes.

"If that's not enough—what if you hurt me? I can tell you right now, I will initiate a suit against you. Should my injury be severe, this flight could be jeopardized. Look around this plane. Do you want to hurt all these people sitting here?

"If I were you, I would think very carefully. You will be subject to arrest. You will be endangering this airplane. Now if swinging at me is worth risking all that, then go ahead, swing—I won't try to deter you from it."

According to the stewardess who was witness to this cameo and who told me about it later in a Coral Gables lounge, the woman in fur hardly hesitated a moment. She just drew back her fist and knocked him right on his hindquarters.

In the years since that incident, I've had a lot of time to think about it. I've listened to lectures on psychology and management procedures. I've read what I can about "Cockpit Resource Management," and I've tried to apply it, not just to piloting, but to passenger handling. And the conclusion I've reached is that it's a little like a chess game strategy. As captain, you're king. You're a god, but you're vulnerable. If your foe checks your king, you're in a very serious chess dilemma. The king is supreme, but you need pawns to protect him sometimes.

Let's take another look at that incident, and this time let's see how the captain *might* have handled it:

As it happened that day, we had a rather dubious weather outlook. We were flying into storms. We could have had turbulence and lightning facing us. I, as first officer, was perfectly well qualified, but the loss of his leadership could have proved incalculably dangerous for us. He had two other crewmen. We were both there and able-bodied. He could have sent either back. He could have asked me to deal with it; he could have said to the F/E, "We've got a problem with a woman back there. Go and see what it's about. Come back and give me a briefing on it."

But that's not what he did. What he did was "take charge" of matters. He wasn't injured—she didn't break any bones or anything—but he was clearly at variance with sound resource management, and had the "she" been a "he" it could have proven disastrous for us.

Ever since then, I've tried to utilize my "chess game strategy." When a passenger acts up, I'll send a pawn back to deal with it. If the pawn doesn't work, then I'll send back a bishop. Only as a very last resort will I myself get involved in it.

Of course there have been exceptions.

It was a 6 P.M. flight, and we were leaving from La Guardia. We had just closed the door and were pulling away from the passenger gate. It was a holiday period, and we were wall-to-wall people. The flight was to Orlando, and we had all these vacationers flying with us.

The phone suddenly rang. It was one of our flight attendants. I was taxiing the plane, and I was worried about delay problems. I was not in any mood to take a call from a flight attendant saying she had a couple back there and they were smoking pot in the lavatory.

Jesus Christ spare me, I thought.

Pot in the lavs. You probably think I'm inventing this. We've had people on planes who have actually screwed in those lavatories. A few years ago there was a fraternal organization that had high-altitude orgasm as one of its membership requirements. We've had passengers who have "streaked." We've had women put negligees on. We've had people use the lavatories for cocaine fixes and crack smoking. Eastern, I believe, had a celebrated case in which a guy in the john was using a blowtorch for free-basing.

So we get all these freaks, and we have to learn how to deal with them. We use a well-tempered mixture of toughness and diplomacy. We do what we can not to tarnish our companies, but our first and top priority is to keep it a safe operation up there.

Under normal conditions I would have pulled out my chess game strategy. I would have played it by the textbook called *Good Resource Management*. I'd have enlisted the help of one of my able-bodied crewmen, who would have promptly gone back and given those fools a good talking-to.

Only this time I couldn't. My crew wasn't "able-bodied." My flight engineer was about five foot seven. My trusty first officer, who was in other ways capable, had a slight disadvantage, in that she had never had judo training.

*Shit.*

So there was nothing else for it. I had to stop, pull the airplane over. I had to park its fat carcass between a couple of baggage carriers. I had to put on my coat and my little hat with the braid all over it and go back to the rear and see if I could try to restore order back there.

Pot in the lavs. I have some news items staring at me. Here's one about a flight in which the passengers started food-fighting. Two of the passengers had been caught having intercourse, and the others responded by standing up and heaving trays at each other. I have another clip here about a guy who threw his knife at somebody. He didn't like his meal—he thought his meat was too rare or something—so he picked up his tray, threw his food at the stewardess, and then he picked up his knife and started slinging it around the passenger cabin. The stories go on. I myself have a file of them.

I had a guy get on board wearing pants with no crotch seams in them. I had to pull him aside and tell him to cover his gonads, or else we'd spend the whole night sitting right there in Boston, damn it. I had a woman on board who tried to pull a false injury claim. After the plane had touched down, she said I had detached her retina. Fortunately for me, the other passengers took my side, and after a couple of days she crawled back beneath the rock she'd come from.

So you can never be sure just what on earth you might find up there. Since the early 1980s most of our lavs have had smoke detectors; but there's always some jerk who decides to light up a Marlboro, plus the occasional wizard who tries to bypass the alarm system.

Anyway—

By the time I got back there, the couple had exited. They had returned to their seats. They looked as innocent as choir members. In fact, if it hadn't been for people turning around and pointing their fingers at them, I wouldn't have had the faintest idea who it was I was supposed to be looking for.

There are a number of things that the captain has prerogative over. He's the airship's commander. He's like a temporary governor up there. He's not only the captain, he's the airline's executive officer. Should circumstances warrant, he can order free rounds of drinks for everybody.

But even a captain has to exercise prudence. What you're trying to do is accomplish an objective. You don't mess with passengers who are looking for trouble, and you don't get into fights, even if you've got God and the court system backing you.

Or at least I don't.

"Excuse me," I said, as I confronted the couple. I leaned across their chairs, so that they were practically pinned to the seat cushions. The young man looked dazed. The girl looked electrocuted. She had wild, frizzy hair and a man's shirt with no underwear under it. "Excuse me," I said, "I'd like to have a brief word with you." They didn't respond. They just sat there and grinned at me. I said, "Play it my way and I'll fly you to Orlando. Play it your way, and you can take a bus down to Disney World."

Well, the two were disconsolate. "Oh no, sir!—forgive us, Captain!"— and so on and so forth—they didn't want to turn back again—so that the impression I had as I returned to the flight deck was that the matter was settled and I'd have no further trouble from them.

End of Chapter One.

The second chapter opened after we had landed in Orlando. We were parked at the gate, and I was saying good-bye to people. I was standing at the door—I had my coat and my hat on—and here comes this guy, and he's got his frizzy-haired girlfriend with him.

"Bye, Cap!" he says, and he starts to come toward me—

—and suddenly he swings!

I was completely astounded. There I am smiling, I've got my hands in my pockets—and my vision suddenly fills with the sight of his fist coming at me!

As it happens, thank God, I am not all that fragile. I'm a middle-aged man, but I have pretty good muscle tone. Moreover, back when, I had a fair amount of combat training, so I feel reasonably confident when confronting an adversary.

As his fist started up, it ran into my forearm. I lifted my left. I took a half-step backward. I planted my feet and drew back with my right. If it was a tussle he wanted, I'd be glad to accommodate him.

"No! Wait!" cried the kid, and he suddenly looked terrified. He lifted his arms. It was as if now he were surrendering to me. For a moment we stood there like a couple of game cocks. I was totally confused, because now he was *smiling* at me.

"You don't understand—I just want to say thank you!" he said, and with that his arm began to relax, and the fingers of his fist began to uncurl, and he dropped into my palm—

—two marijuana cigarettes.

Well, try to put yourself in the place of those airline passengers. You're getting off the plane. You've got your spouse and your children with you. Here's your great captain, Golden Thor of the Skyways—and he's standing with his hand out, and it's got a couple of reefers in it.

"Hey, wait!" I protested—and I tried to take after him, but the kid was too fast—he was gone through that jetway; and there stood yours truly, looking shamefaced and crimson, trying to explain to the public that this was all a bad joke of some sort.

Pot in the lavs. Of course it's not just the riffraff nowadays. As a major line pilot, I've flown numerous famous people. I've flown Newman and Redford. I've had a President-elect fly with me. I've flown all the major athletes from just about all the major sports franchises.

Usually these people are very polite and quite accommodating. They just want their peace. They don't want to be bothered by anybody. But every so often you get a star who's . . . well, difficult. The residue it leaves can be pretty distasteful sometimes.

A colleague of mine was flying a well-known television actress. She was in the first-class section. She was being served by a flight attendant. That poor little hostess was so flustered and nervous—in the act of leaning over she accidently spilled coffee on her.

"Oh, my goodness!" cried the stewardess. "I'm so clumsy . . . I'm sorry, really!" And she began fluttering and dithering and running around to get napkins for her. "Forgive me! Oh, dear! I don't know what's gotten into me! I hope it doesn't stain! Is there anything I can do for you?"

"Yes, dahhhling," said the actress, giving the attendant her best porcelain-bonded dentalwork smile: "You can go back to the kitchen and get me more coffee, dahhhling."

Well, wasn't that nice. So back goes the stewardess. She gets some more coffee, and she hands it to the celebrity. Whereby the actress stands up—and pours it all over the stewardess. "There," says the actress, "now be a deah and take the cup back, dahhhling."

Remember that the next time you see one of those people acting so charming on the Johnny Carson Show.

There was a flight to L.A. It had Bette Davis on it. It was not a nonstop, it had a couple of stopovers. Each time they landed the actress excused herself. She got off the plane and paid a visit to the ladies room.

A stewardess thought perhaps she could be of some help to the celebrity: "Excuse me, Miss Davis—I hate to disturb you, but I notice you get off and use the airports' ladies rooms. I just want to remind you that you don't have to do that. We have bathrooms on board. You can use one of our lavatories."

"My deahhh," smiled the irrepressible Miss Davis: "I am perfectly aware that this airplane has lavatories. But I am also aware of what the passengers do to them. The tissues they leave . . . the garbage and filth all over. . . . It's really quite grim. It makes a terrible impression on people.

"Now imagine how *you'd* feel if you followed me in there. You'd see all that stuff, and you'd say, '*God, what a mess she's made!*' When you're a well-known person, you've got enough image problems. I don't need one more. I'll use the johns in the airport, thank you!"

I always loved Bette Davis before hearing that story, and I love her even more since the day that was repeated to me.

My favorite passenger story is not of a celebrity. It's not of a druggie, and it's not of a crazy person. It's of a planeload of people who were flying to Los Angeles and had to put down in Texas after the plane developed an engine problem.

As it happened that day was a Sunday, and it was football season. The little local airport was as dead as a cemetery. There was no one around. You couldn't even find a newsstand open. If you wanted a drink, too damn bad—there was no booze at that airport.

The passengers on board learned that the damage was serious. A replacement plane would have to be sent in from headquarters. In the meantime there was nothing that the passengers could do about it. They had to make themselves comfortable and find a seat in the terminal somewhere.

Some of the first-class passengers were particularly resourceful. They managed to get some glasses and a liquor bottle from somewhere. They found a couple of seats near a color TV set, turned on the set and became engrossed in an Oilers game.

Now as it happened, that lounge was the property of a commuter line. It had been left in the charge of a particularly dour bureaucrat. This woman had orders to keep people out of there, so she asked them to leave—and, when they wouldn't, she turned their television off.

The passengers were furious. What the hell was this biddy's problem? They were *stranded,* goddamn it! Couldn't she extend a little courtesy to them? And so on and so forth—the shouting grew louder—and finally she responded by calling in the sheriff's office.

At this point the story gets a little more ragged-edged. The sheriff has his side. The passengers have their side.

The sheriff arrives, and he has a couple of deputies with him—and they make the very serious error of trying to confiscate the liquor bottle.

I offer this story as a strange sociology lesson. It used to be trains that brought the odd walks of life together. It used to be steamships. It used to be Greyhound stations. Not anymore—now it's your everyday airline terminal.

When the sheriff took the bottle, it became a challenge to warfare. The fliers grew furious. There were punches and insults hurled. The next thing you know there are arrests being made—and the entire first-class roster is being locked in the sheriff's pokey!

Stories like this are constantly traded among airline people. They're bandied in cockpits. They'll make the rounds of the flight attendants. They'll end up being printed in some newsletter or house organ whose pages get clipped and tacked up on crews' bulletin boards. If the line isn't yours, your response will be gleeful. "Ha ha! Serves 'em right! Poor American . . . or Braniff!" you chortle. But if it happens to be yours, you feel picked on and persecuted. You say, "What the hell's wrong with those damn redneck sheriffs down there!"

In this particular case, the story grew weirder. The plane's tourist class, which had witnessed this episode, began chanting and shouting and heckling the sheriff's office. They cried, "Free the first class!" and began behaving as if they were at a protest rally. Phone calls were made. People began calling the airline headquarters. A new plane was readied, and it was sent out to rescue them, but in the course of setting down one of its food carts got loose, shot the length of the plane, and splintered the door of the flight compartment!

So now this poor airline's got *two* crippled airplanes out there. They've got a first-class roster who will forever hate Texas, and they've got a mean local sheriff who, as far as I know, still holds them responsible for flying a planeload of rabblerousers in there.

Pot in the lavs. When these lines were deregulated, it was decided that everyone should live by free market values. Only one in five people had ever been on an airplane, and they were not the kind of people one would find in a Trailways station. Today all that's changed. Today we get everybody. More than nine out of ten Americans have boarded an airplane sometime. We fly twice as many people on about 70 percent more airplanes, with the overwhelming majority being discount and "Apex" passengers.

That some of these people aren't so nice isn't newsworthy. A little anxiety can make a monster out of anybody. But we get passengers nowadays who are truly demented—as witness this story attributed to a rival airline company:

There was a man we'll call H. He was a New England band director. He was a nice little guy. He had never hurt anybody. He was taking his band from some town in New Hampshire, and they were going to New York, where they were going to march in a St. Paddy's ceremony.

You'll remember what I said about the infamous Excedrin Capitals. Well, also on this plane was a well-dressed Manhattan type. That poor band director was about to encounter "Fun City"—with certain results that would not be too humorous for him.

They had just taken off. The band was excited. This was the first time they had ever even been out of New Hampshire. Here they were, they were going to New York, and there would be parades and excitement and all sorts of dignitaries present.

Suddenly H. spots the aforementioned slicker type. He's back from first class, and he's standing by a lavatory. He has a lascivious leer spread all over his kisser, and he's trying to put the make on one of the sixteen-year-old tuba players!

Oh, for gosh sake! thinks H.

So he unbuckles his seat belt. He puts down his magazine. He gets out of his seat and he goes over to this Manhattanite. He says, "Excuse me, sir, I'm in charge of these students. This girl here is sixteen. I'd like to ask that you not bother her."

The New Yorker says nothing. He's got eyeballs like nerve ganglia. H. goes back to his seat. There's a several-minute interlude. Then, "Excuse me—" says the New Yorker, and he's towering over H. He grabs H. by the lapels—

—and he bites the band director's nose off!

Well, here's one for history. They've got a freak with a nose in his mouth. They've got a band director screaming. They've got torrents of blood all over. They've got all these young high schoolers screaming "Eeeeek!" and "Ooooh, yukkie!"—and this New Yorker turns around and he goes back up to his seat again.

The guys in the cockpit can't believe what's reported to them. "He did *what?*" they keep saying as the stewardess stands babbling at them. She's muttering incoherently about high schools and tuba players and there's blood on the floor and there's some guy who's got no nose left on him.

The payoff to this story is that the New Yorker was a professional man. He was a licensed physician and a closet cocaine addict. When the FBI came and hauled him off to the hoosegow, they found quantities of drugs stuffed down under his seat cushion.

So that's how it is. Today, we tote everybody. We've got yuppies and druggies and alkies and crazy people. And every so often (although only once for yours truly, fortunately) we encounter a passenger who is genuinely terrifying. . . .

## Chapter 11

# The Hijack

You don't hear as often about skyjacks and bombings nowadays. They're still a concern—there was that recent Pan Am disaster—but in the sixties and seventies we had so many incidents that we had to spend millions of dollars on installing new security checkpoints.

There are fewer incidents now, but we still have too many of them. Since planes started flying, there have been 245 hijack attempts. Of these, more than half have ended in failure. Most have been foiled. Some have ended tragically.

My own brush with fate had a surprise happy ending. The plane didn't crash. I'm still here; I'm still talking about it. But at the time it was happening things were not all that certain, and there was no earthly way I could have predicted the outcome.

The flight we were taking was from Detroit to San Francisco. I was in my thirties at the time—I was a fresh-faced first officer. The captain of the plane (and he was the one actually driving it) was a stout, grizzled man whom I'll call . . . Captain Vernal Equinox.

Now I'm calling him that because it reflects how I feel about him. The majority of captains are extraordinarily capable. They've been screened through the strainers both of time and of check-rides, and if they don't pass those tests they don't advance to the commander's position. But every so often you get a bit of a misfit in there. I had been flying with old Vernal for about the past several weeks or so. The guy drove me nuts. He was a bore, and he was arrogant. He was technically proficient, but he was not a good resource manager.

The stewardess that day—I'll never forget how her hands were shaking. Apparently there was a man, and he was sitting in coach class. He had beckoned her over, and he had given her a message. It was that she should go tell the captain that he was in charge of this airplane now.

"And he said he had a bomb?"

The stewardess nodded.

"Did you see where it was?"

"I'm not sure . . ." She stared vacantly at us. Clearly, her mind was too frozen in terror. We were going to have to draw straws and send a man back to investigate it.

There are certain procedures flight crews follow during hijackings. These are FAA classified, and I have no wish to broadcast them. But I can at least point to options that may work in our favor if we can assume that the nut has a modicum of logic left in him.

I mentioned transponders. We can use our transponder numbers. Transponders are programmed by keys on our control consoles. They transmit a signal which is picked up by radar and which flashes a code that appears on the controller's monitor. Each scheduled flight has a specific transponder number. To the men on the ground it is their way of identifying us; if you alter that code by means of predetermined serial numbers you can communicate to ground without using your radio transmitter.

In the flight bags we carry, we have all kinds of flight procedures. People sometimes ask us if we're carrying our laundry in there. In point of actual fact we've got manuals and policy directives—plus a number of "aids" that can be of help in a hijack incident. There's a map, for example. We can hand it to a hijacker. It shows the entire Western Hemisphere, and it's got Cuba in the center of it. If we show him that map, and he's not totally wacko, he can see where we are and whether we have enough fuel capacity.

We don't carry guns, but we've had training in bomb removal. We have foreign language cards by which we can communicate with terrorists. We have procedures for medical and explosive and fire contingencies, and we have classified signals by which we can communicate to SWAT team members.

So we're reasonably well stocked—and a lot better than we used to be. At the time of this incident, all these things were still nascent for us. We could use our transponders, and we could communicate by radio, but that was about it. We were alone and we were vulnerable up there.

I turned to the captain. "What do you think?" I said anxiously.

Vernal just sat there. He was glued to the control column. "Son of a bitch," he kept saying. His eyes glowered angrily. He was hunched in his seat as if this were a race and he was a bobsled driver.

The flight engineer was a young man I'll call Dixon. He was a so-called "new hire." He had seen service as a chopper pilot. It was apparent to me that if we were going to get out of this it was going to have to be Dixon through whom I would have to coordinate it somehow.

"There's that," Dixon muttered.

He was glancing toward the bulkhead. There was a bracket back there. It had an eagle-beaked crash ax mounted on it. These are traditional on planes. I've never had to use one, but in theory they're there to break down doors and get to electrical circuits.

"Good thought," I said, nodding. I reached for our passenger manifest. Before we take off, we get all sorts of passenger info. Among other facts, we're told who's carrying handguns on them. There are mutual introductions, so that they won't mistakenly start shooting at each other.

In this case, we had no armed passengers listed.

A few years ago I was sitting watching television. It was about two in the morning. They were showing old movie reruns. The movie that night was the original film *Airport,* which, as some might recall, was about a plane that's got a bomber loose on it. And as I sat there and watched it, I was reasonably impressed by it. I thought, Hey, this is great—it's good fun, and it's convincing, actually. In fact, if I were somebody other than a man who knows airplanes, I might actually believe that this is the way things would happen up there.

To a pilot, however, it was totally implausible. There were about a half-dozen flaws that seemed to run through the center of it, the most notable being that, at 40,000 feet, if there's a bomb on the plane you don't just stay at that altitude level. How dumb can you be? *C'mon, get that plane down there, dummy!* You've got to bring your plane down to about 10,000 feet or so. When the explosive goes off (and you just know that's going to happen, don't you?), you'll have a hole in your plane, but at least you won't lose your flight attendants through it.

Well, I'm happy to report that at least *we* weren't that simpleminded. My old buddy Vernal had some warts on his character, but he at least knew enough to send a message to the control center and start to nose the plane over so that we could get our damn pressure equalized.

This plane, as it happened, was a DC-8 turbojet. In that pre-dereg era it had a couple of amenities on it. One of those touches was a small first-class passenger lounge that had aft-facing seats and a table to put your cocktails on. The scheme we concocted was that I'd walk back and talk to the guy. I'd try to lure him forward and get him to sit in the passenger lounge. Once he was there, and he had his back to the flight-deck entrance, out would jump Dixon and drive the ax through his cerebral hemispheres.

It's what, in retrospect, I'd call the left brain/right brain method of hijack control.

So that's what we did. I unhooked my safety harness. I exited the flight deck wearing my neatly pressed shirtsleeves . . . and only then did it occur that, when you're going to meet a hijacker, you might want a little something that will leave you less naked feeling. So on my way past the galley I picked up a paring knife. It had about a two-and-a-half-inch blade, and it was the kind you cut lemons with. I wiped off the fruit rind, threw a glance at a flight attendant, and tucked the knife down inside the back of my trouser waistband.

I suppose what I expected, as I view this in retrospect (and how grateful I am that I've been permitted to view it that way! In a minute I'm going to tell you about another dire incident in which, when the dust finally settled, things were not all that salutary)—I suppose what I expected is that I'd be able to intimidate him. I'd draw myself up, give him my best John Wayne sergeant look, and the guy would just fold. He'd become a tub of gelatinous matter. I'd get a bonus from my company, plus a couple of presidential citations.

That's what I expected. That is not what took place, unfortunately. What took place was an exchange that was a little more sobering. As I made my way back, I could see the guy smiling at me. He looked totally composed. I could feel my own pulse rate quickening.

"Got a problem?" I asked.

"Not at all," the man answered. He was thin, blond-haired, balding. He had gray eyes like ball bearings. He had a woman beside him. She looked absolutely terrified.

He just smiled at me coolly.

"It's *you* got the problem," he told me.

I would not be the last. There was a captain named Loftin. He was flying out of Baltimore, and they were sitting at the passenger gate. It was seven in the morning, and he had his copilot with him. Suddenly they were aware that there was an intruder in the door behind them.

This tale-within-a-tale may sound vaguely familiar to you. At the time that this happened it was almost buried under news calamities. It was 1974, and the headlines were dizzying. It was a day ruled by demons, and this story is of one of those demons.

On that same winter morning, we were in the heart of the Watergate scandal. Nixon was bunkered. They were gathering impeachment evidence. There were long lines of cars waiting to get gas at all the gas stations. The nation was reeling. We were like a ship, and there was no captain manning us.

As the little shards of madness began to break from the capital, shooting like spears throughout that bleak, winter landscape, they had made their appearance in the oddest of places, as if some glue had dissolved and there was nothing cohesive holding us. Patty Hearst was still missing. They were offering a $4-million ransom for her. Riots had broken out over the Symbionese Liberation Army food dispersal program. An editor named Reg Murphy had been abducted in Atlanta. A soldier with a helicopter had tried to barnstorm the White House earlier.

At Baltimore-Washington International, which had formerly been called Friendship Airport, and where a Delta DC-9 was in the midst of a boarding procedure, a man with a gun had rushed in, shot a security guard, then run toward the plane carrying a case that had gasoline dripping from it.

To young Charlie Troyer, who was with the Anne Arundel Police Department, and who was moonlighting that day in order to supplement his patrolman's salary, the sound of those shots was like the sound of aluminum snapping. He had just ordered coffee at a stand in the terminal building.

As Troyer recalls, there was immediate chaos. People were running. There was a veritable stampede in front of him. Everyone was yelling—apparently somebody had shot somebody—but who had shot whom, and was the gunman among the people running?

When he got to the B Pier, it was blocked by a security gate. This was the area that everyone was running from. The impression Troyer had was that it like was some sort of dream unfolding. There was a guard on the floor. There was blood, and there were people screaming.

"Down there!" someone shouted. They were pointing toward the passenger gate. Troyer thought fast. He had a .38 service revolver. The guard on the floor had a .357 magnum on him. Troyer holstered his gun and quickly picked up the dead man's pistol.

In Doug Loftin's memory, it would all seem suspended somehow. His copilot, Fred Jones, had just reached for his pipe tobacco. Jones was thirty-two years old. He was small, and he was balding. A couple of days earlier they had taken some stewardesses and gone bowling together.

As Loftin remembers, Jones was feeling quite good that morning. A day or so earlier he had received a check from his credit union. He had a couple of kids, and they had congenital eye problems. The check he had gotten was going to go toward an eye operation.

To Loftin, of course, there would naturally be blank spaces. Trauma does that: it destroys the connective tissue. It eats away the context, leaving isolated images, so that when you try to look back you can't really make sense of anything. But he'd remember the voice. There would be something about the White House shouted. A gun would appear. It would look comic and outsized to him. The next thing he knew there would be a puff from the barrel. He could actually *see* the bullet as it leaped from the firing chamber.

At the end of the passage, Troyer was running toward the airplane entrance. There was an agent near the jetway. The agent was screaming at him. Troyer dashed through. He heard a slam—and then a click behind him. The agent had locked the door! Troyer was being trapped with some maniac in here!

As Loftin sat spellbound, the bullet kept traveling. It sped the few feet between the gun and the copilot. It entered Jones's head between the ear and the temple. It exploded in a geyser, splattering blood down the instrument panel.

The next thought that mattered was that it was about to become Loftin's turn. "Fly!" the man said. "I ca—!" Loftin protested, but before he could finish a slug pierced his shoulder. It ran down his chest and turned to shrapnel in his midsection.

As it happened that morning, there were three working flight attendants. Two were up front. One was in the tourist section. There was a handful of passengers, but the plane wasn't crowded yet; the majority of people had never made it past the security entrance.

"Get down!" Troyer shouted. He was shouting at two flight attendants. They were standing in the doorway. They were blocking the airplane entrance. Troyer hunched down, waved the muzzle of his pistol at them. He could see the man he wanted, but he couldn't get a shot off at him.

Troyer's memory would have it that he was shouting at white women. Another mirage. Both the women were black. He would be surprised to learn that later when he looked at the news photos. But then nothing that day would be remembered the way the records showed it.

*"Get out of the way!"*

And now they both lowered. Only they weren't ducking down—they were wrestling with the door handle. They were closing the door and trapping the killer in the airplane! Great . . . good idea . . . only now he had a door in front of him!

In the rear of the plane there was nothing but chaos reigning. There was a third flight attendant, and she had eight or ten passengers back there. The man with the pistol kept running back and grabbing people. He'd drag them up front and make them kneel in the cockpit area.

"Fly!" he told Loftin.

"I can't!" Loftin protested.

The passengers were weeping. There was a girl, and she was praying to him. She was down on her knees, and she was sobbing hysterically. The man cocked his gun and held it pressed against her occipital bone.

What Loftin assumed—and it was a valid assumption—was that if they pulled from the gate there would be no way of rescuing them. Once in the air, they would have lost all their leverage. He had no misconceptions about what this madman's intentions were.

To keep that from happening, Loftin formulated a game plan. He would try to make a case that they were being held there for technical reasons. He was bleeding profusely, but he continued to temporize: The doors weren't closed tight . . . they needed clearance from the control tower . . .

"Look! It won't go!"

He began revving the engines up. The plane bucked and heaved. The noise was excruciating. That it indeed wouldn't go was not really that surprising, since he had his foot on the brakes, and he had the jets in the "reverse-thrust" position.

Among other passengers whom the madman dragged up there with him and whom he commanded to kneel so that he could intimidate the pilot was a middle-aged woman who was the wife of an Army sergeant. Only she was not the kind of woman to accede to such temper tantrums.

"Now, see here—" she told him, and she began verbally upbraiding him. The gunman just stood there. He seemed totally nonplussed by her. He had just killed two people, and he was about to kill a third one, but here was this woman, and she was delivering a sermon to him!

Troyer, in the meantime, was learning about airplane tires. When he heard those jets roaring, he had immediately begun panicking. To him it was a sign that they were trying to get out of there; and he knew that, if they did, there would be no way of rescuing them.

So he had rushed down some stairs. He was out on the tarmac now. He had drawn both his guns and he had begun firing at the airplane tires. Only the bullets just bounced. They became imbedded in the airplane body. Those tires are steel-belted, and they have 28-gauge tire tread circling them.

"Hey you! Bring that shotgun!"

There was a guard, and he had a shotgun with him. The two stood together. They began firing at the airplane tires. With magnum and shotgun, they tore through the sidewalls. The huge tires exploded like so many bombs exploding.

"Son of a bitch!" Loftin murmured. He was marveling at this Army woman. Being a typical pilot, Loftin tended toward chauvinism. But here was this . . . *female* . . . showing absolute coolness, and from the corner of his eye he could see the man's gun arm lowering.

By now, Loftin's vision was beginning to grow dimmer. Later he'd liken it to "looking through toilet paper rollers." He had lost so much blood, he was practically unconscious. But hurt as he was, he still had an option open.

The stouthearted woman was giving the gunman a civics lesson. She was calling him a fool—and the gunman was listening to her! It began to appear that he might actually put the gun down! If Loftin could turn and get his hands on that gun barrel . . .

Having shot out the tires, Troyer ran up the stairs again. On those DC-9 planes, the main door has a porthole in it. Troyer ran to the porthole and leveled his pistol at it. *C'mon, man . . . c'mooon* . . . If he could just get his gunsights on him. . . .

Just about then, Loftin lunged for the gun barrel. And it was also about then that there was a scream from another passenger. The gunman snapped to. Loftin turned, made a grab for it—

—and only then did he realize that he still had his seat belt buckled!

The third flight attendant had finally opened a window exit. She was jumping to the wing. The passengers were following her. When they finally hit ground, there'd be a couple of injuries, but there'd be nothing to match what was happening to that airline pilot.

Loftin held on. He was clenched to that gun barrel. By the time this was over, he would have four gaping bullet holes in him. The bullets were "dumdums." Most were in his midsection. One was in his hand. One shoulder would be paralyzed. . . .

"C'mon mannnnn," thought Troyer. He was standing at the passenger door. Through the hole in the door he could see the aisle and the lavatory entrance. There was a movement of shadow. He drew bead, cocked the pistol hammer. Time seemed to freeze. It was like the stillness of death descending.

Finally, inexorably, the killer yanked backward. Loftin let go. The man spun, turned away from him. As he twirled toward the rear, he saw the gun at the porthole. He wheeled, gave a cry, tried to duck into the lavatory.

The magnum rang out. Three slugs pierced the lavatory. The first bullet missed. It passed out through the airplane body. The second and third drilled two holes in the plywood, splintered the door—and caught the man in the chest cavity.

The coroner's report would be somewhat confusing afterward. It would mention both slugs as being potentially fatal. Yet the bullet that killed him was a third, final bullet that was found in his head and that was apparently self-administered.

As to who this man was, that they'd also learn subsequently. He was a Philadelphia ex-tire salesman. He had become distraught over the Watergate scandal. He had dictated a tape to Jack Anderson, the newspaper columnist, saying that he was going to hijack a plane and fly it straight into the Oval Office.

As for Jones, he was dead. So was the security guard. Doug Loftin was critical. He would spend five years recovering from it. When the medics arrived they piled him onto a helicopter, where he lay smiling at the nurse.

"Did I do it okay?" he asked her.

It's these kinds of stories that make the rounds among airline circles. They're told and retold. They become smooth from the telling of them. And every pilot listening wonders how he would have handled it, and would he have "done it okay," and would he have managed to bring honor on himself. In this particular instance, I think the answer is obvious. Doug Loftin is still flying. He's out in the Pacific somewhere. I can picture him now, winging his way to Korea, just waiting for some fool to try to come and take his airplane away from him.

There are men, I imagine, who will know how I felt right then. It's when you go to face someone, and you throw down a challenge to him. Only the guy that you're challenging doesn't mind being challenged. He responds in a way that makes your blood turn to ice water.

The thing I remember was the seeming inhumanness of it. He was so damn composed! I could feel all my sweat glands opening. I was standing in this airplane with two miles of space beneath me, and I could feel my heart racing as if it were tied to one of those engines out there.

"Would you like," I said dryly, "to come up and talk about it?"

The bomber just shrugged. He could afford to be charitable. We were all in his power. There was nothing we could do about it. He could come up and talk—or he could just blow the plane from around us.

Earlier I mentioned that there's a device that you can communicate with. It's called a transponder. It sits on the control console. It has a four-digit number through which your flight is identified, and if you alter that code you can tell ground that you've got a hijack in progress. When your signal is received, you'll be patched through to headquarters. There, down below, they'll establish a crisis center. Your Flight Control team will begin to swing into action. The word will go out: *We've got an airplane in trouble up there.*

These Flight Control centers are in themselves rather interesting. They're long, darkened rooms. They have acoustical upholstery in them. When an airplane's in trouble, they can patch through to experts, including police and psychiatrists—even the men who built the airplane for you. The first consideration is the safety of your passengers. If you need to reach State, they'll put you through to the State Department. If you need the man's mother, by God they'll get the creep's mother for you. They'll do everything they can to try to stabilize the atmosphere up there.

All that was happening even now as I was standing there. Hundreds of people would be alerted and frantic over us. For which I was grateful—it was all we had going for us—but I'd have been happier still if I could have been down there where they were sitting.

The bomber stood up. I turned, began walking. I started, as planned, to lead him up to the passenger lounge. But only then did I realize that, in turning my back on him, I was showing the knife that was still stuck in my trouser waistband!

I record this in memory of all those who came after me: The pilots, now dead, who were murdered by terrorists . . . the pilots who kept flying, veering from country to country, while cowardly governments continued to dicker over them. If they were soldiers or cops, they'd have been cited for bravery. Soldiers and cops get the nod from political leaders. Airline crews don't. It's just accepted as "duty." What in others seems brave is just part of our job requirement.

"After *you,*" I said quickly. I held out my hand for him. Again the man shrugged—he was perfectly accommodating. It was as if nothing he granted was going to alter the outcome of it. We were all going to die. We were just there to provide amusement for him.

By now certain facts had begun to seep through to me. If the guy had a bomb, it was certainly not visible on him. He was carrying no case; there was no bulge in his coat pocket; he had nothing in his hands that might be taken to be a trigger mechanism.

But what did I know?—he could have had something in the cargo hold. He could have had something near his seat, or in a lav, or in a coat compartment. This was back there in the days before our tightened security systems. As far as I knew, he could have even had an accomplice helping him.

Our tightened security. A word on that subject: Our security at airports isn't as tight as it's supposed to be. In 1988, twenty-nine U.S. airlines were fined $1.6 million for failure to detect guns that the FAA was smuggling past them. But on a relative basis, the deterrent is effective. We find 88 percent of all FAA-planted firearms. That's a pretty good percentage, and an obstacle to hijackers—the more so when coupled with sure and lengthy prison sentences.

"Now tell me," I said when I had gotten him to the passenger lounge and he was sitting in a seat and had his back to the flight-deck entrance; through the crack in the door I could see shadows and metal flickering; that would be Dixon, ready to pounce and make pork chops out of him— "So tell me," I said, "what can we do to be of help to you?" I was determined to keep talking for as long as the guy would listen to me. What is it they say?—when you're in the hands of a madman you'll do anything you can to try to keep a connection going?

Finally, disjointedly, the man began rambling. It was a strange, garbled story. I couldn't make out the logic of it. There were KGB agents . . . the CIA was involved with it . . . and what he was demanding from us was that we take him to *Canada* somewhere!

"To *where?*" I said, squinting.

"*Now!*" he said, scowling at me. He seemed truly alarmed. His hands had begun trembling. He was demanding, quite adamantly, that we take him to . . . *Winnipeg!* "*Now! Right away!* There's a bomb! They've got agents after me!"

I suppose even then it took a while to sink in completely. His sudden transformation was so quick, unanticipated. From a cool-as-ice killer, he had suddenly become a . . . cry baby! The tears started flowing, and he began sobbing uncontrollably.

"Jeezus Chriiist!" I exploded as I strode through the cockpit, the door bursting open and hitting the end of Dixon's fire ax handle—"Can you believe this?" I ranted. "We got a sonofabitchin loony-tune! He's a fucking bloody hoax! He's just sitting there whimpering at me!"

My relief at this knowledge, although at the time much appreciated, was quickly abated by what I saw through the windshield panels: for there, coming at me, at about the level of our nose cone, was the city of San Francisco, and we were about to plow into the middle of it!

*"Jesus Christ!"* I cried, blanching.

*"Son of a bitch!"* shrieked Captain Equinox. He was hunkered on the stick. He was shouting maniacally. *"Try to blow up my airplane . . . Lemme at him—I'll kill the fucker!"*—and other such rantings. He had become completely unhinged, the dodo!

How we ever made it through and didn't crash that damn airplane I'll never be sure—it's still an enigma to me. We zoomed across the bay at about 500 feet. If we had come in any lower, we'd have hit the San Mateo Bridge uprights.

We sailed toward the runway. We came in like a comet falling. We bounced . . . we flew up . . . we bounced back . . . we flew up again. . . . We came slithering to a halt, almost annihilating some runway markers, and there we sat groaning while the captain gnashed his dentures at us.

In the meantime, on the ground, there had been a firestorm of chaos gathering. The field had been alerted. They knew that we had some sort of bomb emergency. They had instructed our captain to drive straight out the runway and shut the plane down—he was not even to come to the concourse area. Great. Very clever. Only those DC-8 models, you either go to the gate or else you lose all your generator power. They don't come equipped with auxiliary power units, and once you shut down you become a well-upholstered pizza oven.

While that was going on, miles away, near the terminal building, the dust started flying: it looked like some sort of Indian uprising. Every imaginable vehicle—herds of police cars and engine pumpers—was coming our way, and they all had their sirens wailing.

Follow this action: They boarded the airplane. They spotted the culprit. He was sitting there blubbering at them. A group of FBI agents—there were at least a half-dozen of them—promptly threw him to the floor and began pommeling the daylights out of him.

"Take it easy!" I shouted.

"Shut up!" cried the agents.

They were picking him up. They were dragging him down the passenger stairs. The last time I saw him, he was being slung in a station wagon. He was kicking and screaming, and the agents were still wrestling with him.

The end of this story is about as strange as the beginning of it. We were now in a plane that had 160 people on it. We were stranded on a spot that was miles away from the terminal, and we didn't have power, so we'd have to call and get buses out there.

"Excuse me, young man . . ."

She was a little old grandmother type. She wore a flowered straw hat, and she had a suitcase and an umbrella with her. She was standing in the aisle, and she was tugging on my shirtsleeve. I was trying mentally to compute how many buses we should radio for.

"Excuse me," she said.

"Yes, ma'am." I looked down at her.

"Did I understand right, that there's a *bomb* on this airplane?"

"Well, I wouldn't say tha—"

". . . And that the reason we're sitting here is that we're waiting for a bus to come and take us to that terminal over there?"

"Well, yes, ma'am," I said. I didn't really want to *lie* about it. I tried to assure her we had everything accounted for. If she would just remain quiet and go back to the seat assigned her . . . we were doing all we could, and we would soon have some buses out there.

"You're *kidding!*" she told me. She stared at me blankly. She gathered her bags. She picked up her umbrella. She trotted down the stairs that had been left at the doorway, and she began the long march across the field toward the terminal area.

Which was about all they needed. It was like some sort of Bedouin migration. One hundred and sixty people, carrying tote bags and baby strollers, exited that plane and walked clear across the airfield. They just dared any planes to try to take off or land on top of them.

"Well, what do you think?"

I stood staring at Equinox. He had the mike in his hand. He was about to radio for a bus company.

We stood looking about the plane. We were the only ones left out there.

"Aw, fuck it," he muttered.

It was one hell of a long walk, I'll tell you.

# Chapter 12

## Coffee, Tea, or Me II

Between the pilot and the passengers, between the food and dyspepsia, between the arrival of your scotch and going stark, raving bonkers, stand a brave crew of stalwarts commonly known as "stewardesses," but who, for some years, have preferred to be called "flight attendants."

When I first started flying everybody knew what a stewardess was. She was twenty-three years old. She was single, and she was marriage-hungry. She had a service expectancy of about a year and a half, at the end of which time she'd either be pregnant or engaged to somebody. In the parlance of that era, we used to call her a "menu item." That wasn't very nice, but that was the world in which we functioned back then. We'd say, "What's on the menu?" "Well, I might try Denise this evening"—or "Caroline looks nice"—or "I think I'll have a nice blonde this turnaround."

Needless to say, those days are long gone and over now. Not only for me, but for the rest of the industry. We live in an age that's more "enlightened" and dignified. I just hope I may be forgiven if I express some mixed feelings over it.

These people called "stews" didn't start off as sex objects. They started as *men*. They were copilot/baggage handlers. When a seaplane came in, they'd jump off, tie a line to something, then run into town and try to scare up some food for everyone. It was a guy named Steve Stimpson who first got the "stewardess" brainstorm. He was an employee at Boeing. He saw it as a promotion gimmick. He memoed his boss, suggesting that they hire some young nursing graduates, and within a couple of months they had become the hit of the airline industry.

One's view of these women and of the women who followed them (the mode reached its peak during the late 1960s sometime; service was "in," and we were vying for "jet-setters"; with the change of morality we had some pretty wild stewardess rosters)—one's view of these women tended to depend on the evaluator. To men they were targets. To wives they were homewreckers. To pilots like me, they were a source of ambivalence: I was glad they were there, but I considered them an irritant sometimes.

Had you known one and dated her, and had you visited her "domicile" —a small, shared apartment stocked with three-ounce-size liquor bottles— she'd have given you peanuts that said American or United on them, and you'd have found steak in the fridge smuggled home in airsickness pouches. Some of these girls made a science of husband-hunting. They'd keep little notebooks. They'd have the names of male passengers in them. They'd jot down brief musings on politics and stock values so that they would appear to be "informed" should a VIP start chatting with them.

There was a black girl I knew who kept a book on all the men she'd bedded. Among its vast entries were some pretty important political figures. The rumor at the time was that she was moving to New York, where she was going to try to find a publisher and see if she could make a big killing out of it.

One of my more interesting encounters was on a flight from Jamaica. We were flying out of Kingston and heading to La Guardia. On the way to the plane, we got caught in a thundershower. All us pilots were soaked. As we walked, you could hear the water squishing.

When we got on the plane we closed the cockpit door behind us. We took off our shoes. We pulled off our uniforms. We hung our wet duds from various trim tabs and window handles, and when the wheels left the ground we were wearing nothing but our Jockey shorts.

After ten or fifteen minutes there was a knock on the entry door.

"Come in," said the captain.

It was a stewardess. She was from the first-class section.

"I just wondered," she asked, "if you'd all like some coffee up here."

"Sure . . . sure, why not?"

We sat studying our flight material.

The cockpit door closed. A couple of minutes passed.

Again:

Knock, knock, knock!

"Yeah, come in!" we all chorused.

This, too, was a stewardess. She had been working the coach-class gal-ley. Did that coffee take cream? Would we like a little Danish possibly?

I can't swear for sure how many girls that plane had that morning, or who they all were, or whether they were all Miss America contestants, but whoever they were, they all came up personally, and by the time we had touched down we had had about twelve different breakfasts served to us.

When things started changing was after the civil rights brouhahas. In the early 1970s, there was a series of court cases. Judgments were brought against the various airlines concerning stewardesses' age and their inequi-table working conditions. Polls at the time showed that passengers backed the airlines: the predominantly male clients liked their girls young and eligible. They weren't too enamored with being waited on by housewives, and they were certainly not entranced with various child care and preg-nancy issues.

However that was, the courts backed the working women. "Stews" were now out. Suddenly we were dealing with "flight attendants." And many of the servers weren't too strong in the estrogen department. The rear that got pinched was as likely to be a masculine one.

It was soon after that that we faced our first medical crises. The appear-ance of AIDS followed a rampage of herpes viruses. Together, these scourges greatly altered our lifestyles. They also brought changes in poli-cies toward passenger service.

There was a flight from San Francisco. One of the passengers had a fainting spell. The flight attendant in charge performed mouth-to-mouth resuscitation on him. Only after she had performed it did she learn from his traveling companion that the man she had treated was a terminally ill AIDS victim.

Of course AIDS, as we know, is not transmitted that easily, but experi-ences like that have made our companies grow wary. Medical packets are now equipped with certain AIDS protections, including surgical gloves and a CPR breathing cannula.

More effective than AIDS, and more polarizing than feminism (I don't mean to link them, but I'm speaking as a pilot now), we have also been chastened by the very same statute that's created such problems for our maintenance and our scheduling departments.

Namely, deregulation.

To understand why, you have to understand our flying schedules. Before deregulation, we had plenty of playing time. We'd fly a few hours, we'd set down in some town or other, then we'd go to our rooms and we'd have a little fun that evening. It was all very cozy. And we'd have all sorts of schedule leeway. We wouldn't fly again until a day or two afterward. Even when we did, we'd have the very same flight crew with us. We'd be bonded for weeks. We'd become very familiar with each other.

Today when we fly it's a whole different atmosphere. We'll have four flights a day and maybe time for two telephone calls. We're constantly shuttling between crew desk and cockpit, and each leg we take we've got an unfamiliar flight crew flying with us.

The result of all this is that we don't get to know each other. We get very little sleep (and that of the noisy-hotel variety), so that even if by chance we happen to meet some young sexpot, it doesn't do us much good because we're too bloody tired for anything.

At least we captains are. I can't speak for oversexed flight engineers.

Of course there's also the fact that not all stewardesses are youthful nowadays. Many are married, and some of them are grandmothers. We'll have women serving drinks who are lawyers and stockbrokers. Many look upon flying as a sort of lucrative form of moonlighting.

Depending on the carrier (and there can be an enormous disparity here; the profitable lines pay their women quite generously; the ones that are struggling have multi-tiered pay scales, which either may or may not have eventual parity built into them)—depending on the carrier, the work can be profitable. An experienced F/A can make up to $50,000. She has unlimited travel; she has medical and pension benefits. And she's getting all that on a twenty-hour workweek schedule.

The result of such perks is that we have a new breed of flight attendant. Gone is the bird we called the Featherheaded Hubby-Catcher. In her place is a genus of down-to-earth female whose no-nonsense ways can be both fascinating and frustrating.

There's the woman, for instance, we call the *Slam-Clicker*. The Slam-Clicker is a flight attendant who is usually in her thirties. She is most often married. She is likely to have children. She looks on her job as a kind of respite from bone-weariness.

When a beautiful Slam-Clicker leaves the plane for a layover, she'll get in a limo and go to the room assigned her. She'll turn to the pilots, say, "Good night, nice to meet you fellas"—then, *slam*, close the door, and, *click*, shove the bolt behind her.

It's enough to make you cry.

We pilots, of course, are depressed by Slam-Clickers. They'll spend the whole day watching game shows and soap operas. Heaven, to a Clicker, is a hotel room with room service. She'll lie in the tub and won't come out until her flight is leaving.

Another type of stewardess is the one who works "red-eyes." "Red-eyes," or "rockets," are the o'pitchdark-thirty flights. Often these women are the junior-most flight attendants, but there will also be some who actually prefer to work hours like that.

The "red-eye" attendant will feed her kids and clean the dishes afterward. She'll drive to the airport and fly to Chicago. She'll sit around O'Hare, leave again after midnight, and be home in Webster Grove in time to rustle up eggs for everybody.

It's a hell of a schedule. I don't know how she survives it, frankly. It's not just the hours, it's the fact that she's a working mother. But, from her point of view, it has several great virtues: She has time for the kids, and she makes a hell of a good salary out of it.

There's another kind of woman who's been dubbed *Senior Mama*. This is in reference to her rank and also her experience level. A wise Senior Mama is too old to have illusions. She knows just what's what, and she imparts it to the women under her.

When a flight attendant's hired, she'll be bestowed with a seniority number. This will dictate her pay and her rank in the bidding order. The higher her number, the less popular the flights she'll garner. She can forget San Francisco. She's going to get those 2 A.M. Oshkosh beauties.

Depending on the airline, there may be flights that will be barred to her. Certain great flights will be controlled by the senior people. No younger woman is going to fly to Nairobi; there are just too many seniors waiting in line to see Safari Country.

One popular run is any flight to Hawaii. Not only is it warm and filled with luaus and surfer ambiance, it's also desirable because it piles up the flight time. Long ocean flights are much more lucrative than puddle-jumpers.

Since the senior-most staffers tend to dominate these turnarounds, and since they are likely to be women who are past the half-century mark, on a number of airlines (at least up front, where the pilots are sitting), the women on these flights are called the "Hawaii Five-O" contingent.

Not to be confused with one's rank in the seniority system, and the runs you might get, or your pay, or your flying hours, there's another kind of order that's imposed on all flight attendants, and it comes in the form of the "purser," or "head flight attendant."

As is readily apparent, every flight is a business. Liquor is sold. There are staffing and equipment problems. Somebody has to be there to handle the inventory and to check the attendance and tote up the booze sale tallies. This is the job of the purser, or head stewardess. Her pay will be more—she'll have a bit of seniority under her—but since her hours are longer and she has more responsibility, the post she commands is not always a coveted one.

Sometimes these women will also have "Mama" tendencies. That is, being older, they're unimpressed by pilots' lover prowess. They'll warn the young women not to hike up their dresses and not to stoop with their rears in the direction of the flight engineer.

Among pilots, of course, the "easiest" women are Earth Women. There are females on this planet to whom pilots are irresistible. They'll do every bit as much to gain the attentions of a pilot as a groupie might do to gain the favors of a rock performer. But when the woman is a stew, one's élan quickly vanishes. Now that damn pilot is just another male mouth to feed. He's immature, selfish—he's probably paying alimony—and the more senior the woman, the more likely she is to be suspicious of him.

In a moment I'm going to tell you one of my "sex-in-the-cockpit" stories. We all love these stories—they make the *National Enquirer* headlines. But before I do that I want to touch on a topic that remains controversial, even among airline people.

The fearsome allegation that the HIV AIDS virus was carried out of Africa by a man with Air Canada is but the latest accusation in a series of calumnies that have been continually leveled at our nonfemale flight attendants. Actually, these men come from all sorts of backgrounds. Many of them are straight. A few of them are pilot aspirants. Like most airline workers, they just love to be near airplanes. They'll do anything they can to avoid working in an office environment.

Not unlike boys who have signed up for Vassar, figuring it's a great education, and so what if Yale rejected them, many of these guys have had to take a lot of ribbing. The pronouns applied to them are, in most cases, feminine ones. Many older pilots are both baffled and offended by them. "Light in the loafers" will be one slur you'll hear against them. "Great Airborne Fruit Loops" . . . "ball-bearing stewardesses" . . . The insults are many—and we pilots are epithet-happy.

To put this in perspective: When you're talking about flight attendants, you're talking about workers who are *always* underestimated. The public tends to see them as glorified cocktail servers. The public doesn't know all the discipline and the training they've gone through.

Go, as I've gone, to some of the flight attendants' training schools. Watch these young people as they report for orientation meetings. Their eyes are agog. Their heads are full of fantasy. They see themselves as entering the Fun-Loving Airline Industry. Little do they know what the next month will hold for them. Many of them arrive full of women's magazine notions. It's never occurred to them that they might actually have to learn something. Some will be gone by the time the third day is over.

The first big surprise is when they learn about safety factors. Most of these kids thought that flight attendants were cocktail vendors. It's a shock when they're told that, in the event of an emergency, it's *they* who will remain while everyone else gets the hell out of there.

To further that cause, they have to learn about evacuation techniques. The doors on a plane are extraordinarily dangerous. They weigh hundreds of pounds, and they're "armed" with escape chutes. They can break you in two if you don't know what you're doing with them.

It's not just the skills—you have to learn to *command* people. These trainees are young. They may be dealing with business executives. They've got to get some big honcho to haul his ass off a seat cushion and help them free up an exit or else they're all going to perish in there.

Each airline company may fly six or eight airplane types. They'll have 747s. They may have primitive little commuter models. The attendants learn each. They've got to know all the safety equipment. They've got to master the lingo of "girt bars" and "APU torchings."

When they get through with that, and they've learned about food service —(you think you know cooking?—you've got a couple of surprises coming: try to rustle up eggs when you're at 40,000 feet; the things will turn green; this is a whole different environment you're dealing with)—when you've learned about that, you'll get to practice your ditching technique. You'll get to try to inflate a life raft that's about the size of three elephants. Forget about swimsuits—you're going to do this with your street clothes on. And you're going to do it in water, and sometimes at night, and sometimes when it's freezing out.

Earlier I told you about America's "Excredrin Capitals." I told you why it's awful having to deal with New Yorkers. Well, New Yorkers are fun compared with some groups of foreigners. You're going to learn about that in various "intercultural communications" seminars.

Imagine for a moment you're a twenty-year-old flight attendant. You're on your first long-range flight, and it's to Riyadh, Saudi Arabia. You've got 400 passengers. You're on a 747. When they first got on board they looked like well-turned-out resort habitués.

As the flight nears its end, they all duck into the lavatories. Off come the

Guccis. Off come the Blass originals. When they emerge from the john, they'll all be dressed like ayatollahs. They'll look like leftover extras from a *Lawrence of Arabia* outtake.

Recovering from that, you decide to serve a few cocktails to them. Up till then, so you've noticed, they've been regular booze-hounds. But now, all of a sudden, you've got a planeload of teetotalers. Liquor, indeed! How dare you, you infidel!

You can't imagine how much stewardesses love to fly into Moslem country. And then, when they touch down, they're treated like dog meat. As a female, you're dead. You can't even eat meals with your coworkers. You're under virtual "house arrest" until your airplane takes off again.

In an informal survey of a number of flight attendants, we asked, "What are your most and your least favorite layovers?" Below, in no order, is a list of their comments. There's a little something here to offend just about everybody.

*The least favorite destinations are India and South America.*

U.S. flight attendants have trouble with class systems. Latins, they feel, tend to treat them like servants. They also resent having to deal with the "machismo" factor.

Flights to Bombay are, for flight attendants, murder. One trouble with Indians is that they can never say no to anything. The result, say the hostesses, is that you have to be careful: they'll strip your whole galley before you can even get the movie rolling.

*In general, steer clear of the old British Empire.*

The legacy of England is, too often, an insular one. Land in Australia, they'll fumigate your airplane. Set down in Scotland, you've got interminably long quarantine problems.

Conversely, the French are both friendly and civilized. Even in Africa, the difference is noticeable. If the country was French, you'll be treated quite cordially. If it belonged to the Brits, they'll throw a hundred regulations at you.

*The best turnaround is invariably Tokyo.*

The Japanese people are beloved by all flight attendants. "They're so courteous!" they say. "They just sit there and smile at you!" At least that's how they *act*. How they *feel* may be another matter.

There's a consensus among the females that men are nicer than the women passengers. Many women passengers are perceived as "demanding." "They're catty," say the stewardesses. "They're crass." "They don't know anything." Specifically, they feel that women are not as knowledgeable about airline procedures.

Many of these attendants are, of course, older and have been around a while. They've all heard Joan Rivers accuse them of "catering" to the menfolk. And they don't disagree. "It's that we prefer dealing with men," they'll tell you. A frequent-flyer businessman is their most ideal air traveler.

Of course the average airplane passenger is, at heart, fairly decent. One of the problems is that the system puts stress on everybody. If I were a New Yorker, and I had to fight all that tunnel traffic, I'd be pretty shrill, too, and I'd probably feel like strangling somebody.

But the message I carry is: *Please—have some patience, fellas! Try to stay calm—we are not trying to hassle you. You're flying places now that you could have never flown earlier. Stop taking it for granted that a Constitutional guarantee comes with it.*

And now, my famous "sex-in-the-cockpit" story:

It was on a 727. We had four women working. As is common nowadays, we had never met any of them. We were about forty minutes shy of touching down in Chicago when there was a knock on the door. It was one of the flight attendants.

Let me interrupt here to note that, in Chicago, the airport you're dealing with is still the World Champion. It's only "second busiest" by virtue of its flight operations. It's the leader in passengers—and, by far, the leader in delay-hours.

When you're landing in O'Hare, you're landing in a very dense nerve ganglion. Things happen fast. It demands the utmost professionalism. The controllers at O'Hare are the best in the business. They'll say something once, and that's all—you'd better have paid attention to it.

We had three pilots working. We were flying in from Mexico. It was a starry blue night and there wasn't a cloud around anywhere. When the flight attendant knocked, we told her to enter. She soon made it known that she had a "proposition" for us.

Now most flight attendants are notoriously "people people." That's how they're picked. They're gregarious and outgoing. The lines don't like women who come on like Germaine Greer, or who have chips on their shoulders, or who get mad when men make passes at them.

This particular young woman was the soul of such social grace. She was in her mid to late twenties. She was blond and she was beautiful. There was a light in her eyes that gave them a kind of come-hither quality. The word "proposition" took on interesting overtones for us.

My flight engineer was a guy I'll call Slovak. He was twenty-eight or nine. He had seen service as a Navy pilot. Like most flight engineers he was notoriously horny. When the stewardess spoke, you could almost see his ears tilt forward.

Now, I'm not the kind of guy who mixes pleasure with my flying business. I've been known to have fun—I'm certainly no angel; but when I'm involved in a flight, there are just too many dangers. They aren't paying me my salary to mix sex games with landing procedures.

But there was something that night that seemed to bring out the devil in me. The wager, she said, was that they had raised all the toilet seats. They were making a bet that, when we got to O'Hare, we couldn't land the plane without knocking a john seat over.

"Whaddaya bet?" I said, smiling.

The stewardess looked at me. Her eyes never wavered. They were as blue as blue sapphires. She delivered the line as if she were taking a breakfast order:

"What we sort of had in mind was in the nature of a blow job," she told me.

Okay, stop right here. Let's take some time to assess this matter. There's an old pilot joke. It's made the rounds of the airline industry. I'm reminded of it now, because it seems to be relevant. It addresses the way we were probably all staring at her.

The joke goes like this:

## Definition of a Perfect Layover

To a flight engineer the perfect layover is managing not to screw up too badly, plus getting laid by at least two stewardesses before taking off the next morning.

To a first officer, the perfect layover is having the hotel not overcook his steak, plus getting laid by at least one stewardess before taking off the next morning.

To a captain, the perfect layover is having a bowel movement.

Now, I have to admit, that's relatively amusing, and I suppose, all in all, there's a small grain of truth to it. But even us captains are a long way from moribund. I responded to her remark by keying the microphone.

"Chicago, this is ———," I said. "Requesting permission to begin our descent now."

Fortunately, Chicago was in pretty good shape that evening. As I said, it was clear. It was not a big travel weekend. This overstrained mess that

122

we call an air traffic system was, for the moment at least, working more or less efficiently. But at a place like O'Hare you could never be certain. They've got six different runways. They've got hundreds of airplanes down there. During peak travel periods they'll shoot two planes a minute at you. I wanted things cleared so that there would be no sudden surprises sprung on me.

I suppose up to now, if I've left an impression, it's that being a pilot isn't the fun that it used to be. What with deregulation and our too-crowded airlanes, it's like driving a truck. In Times Square. During rush hour. And that's not untrue. The job has become burdensome. A little later on, I'm going to talk about the toll it's taking. Pilots nowadays are among the world's most stressed humans. Our emotional problems are beginning to compete with air traffic controllers'.

But people are people. You can't keep things bottled in you. Even at O'Hare, you have to go for the gusto sometimes. We adjusted our throttles and began to float gently downward. We dropped inch by inch through that clear, moonlit atmosphere. . . .

To get to the point: I grease-jobbed that landing. It was the smoothest damn touchdown in the history of the airline industry. I *dusted* the tarmac. You could have pressed a pair of trousers on it. And I kneaded the brakes as if I were bird walking lily pads.

Behind me, in first class, the passengers applauded. The plane was half-empty. Apparently it was festive back there. Those four flight attendants had managed to turn it into a bachelor party. I just hoped they weren't jabbering about what the stakes of the wager were.

The next thing that happened may require a brief background note. When you're landing an airplane, your cockpit is "sterile." You're not on the phone. You're not worried about passenger problems. Your door is kept closed. You're in the dark, in a cocoon environment.

But even in a cocoon, you're not totally isolated. That door's only plywood. You can hear what people are saying back there. And you can certainly hear a stewardess with her mouth against the partition, shouting, *"So far, so good! Now let's see if you can park it, Captain!"*

If I were to pick one trait that distinguished all flight attendants, I would say it's their spirit. They aren't your pinched-cheek "careerist" types. They look at their job as a means, not an absolute. If they wanted to be Yuppies, they'd have become executives or Wall Street analysts.

But I have to admit, some of these women are characters. They can more than hold their own. They aren't easily buffaloed. And they can certainly stand up to three overeager flyboys landing a plane at O'Hare in search of oral-genital sex fulfillment.

O'Hare, like all airports, has three distinct tarmac sections. First, there's the *runway*. That's a place you don't tarry on. You get off there fast, then you go to the *taxiways*. Once you're through those, you head toward the *ramp* area.

I turned off the runway. I got on a taxiway. The taxiways at O'Hare are like somebody spilled spaghetti out there. They all have funny names. I took the "Inner Scenic" taxiway. I turned at "The Stub." I came back along "Outer Scenic" . . .

We got to the ramp. We began looking for our gate area. At a field like O'Hare there are about 130 passenger gates. Nor are they in order. You'll have Gate Alpha-7, then Gate Alpha-12, with 11 around the corner somewhere. We spotted our gate. We spotted our ramp agent. We knew who he was—he was the one waving flashlights at us. We followed him along, getting closer to the concourse. It was pretty hard to see, so we were dependent upon the signals he gave us.

How can I put this? I wish I could demonstrate it. As you're approaching the gate, the ramp agent is motioning you. He's got a light in each hand. He's waving you forward. With his hands in the air, he looks like a ref giving a touchdown signal.

Then, slowly, methodically, he brings his arms together. You ease off the brake. You're down to mere meters now. His arms form an X . . . and that's it—that's your parking place. And you'd better be stopped, because you can't roll it back again.

Well, that's how this was. He was motioning me forward. I've got Slovak behind me—I could feel the excitement building. I've got four flight attendants, and I can hear them all tittering. The passengers are cheering. The ramp tower's barking at me.

And that's when it happened. I still can't believe it. In twenty years of flying, this was totally unprecedented. For some reason or other—I think there may have been a truck beneath me—the agent gave a start—and then—*slap!*—brought his hands together!

The next sound I heard was like the sound of a lock tumbling. It was like the sound of the Gestapo in the presence of Der Führer. It was like the sound a gun makes when you play Russian roulette with it. It was like the sound—

—oh, so clear—

—of four plastic john seats falling.

People sometimes ask me, "What does it take to become a flight attendant? What are the requirements? Should I encourage my daughter to become one?" (After the abovementioned story, they'll no longer ask that, but there may be some daughters who will show an awakening interest in it.)

Here are some facts:

When a major world airline runs an ad in the paper saying that they're looking for flight attendants, for every hundred applicants there will be fewer than one chosen. In any given year, my line will have more than a hundred thousand flight attendant applications.

In terms of requirements:

You have to be a high school graduate. College is preferred. A foreign language is desirable. Your skin must be clear, your weight must be proportionate, and you have to prove yourself capable during the stress of an employment interview.

Not for the record, but more or less unofficially, they would prefer that the candidate have some prior work experience. Their ideal woman would be in her mid- to late-twenties, having had a couple of years to get her values and her goals in order.

That's what they say. Now I'll give you my personal viewpoint:

What flight attending is is a means to do other things. This is not to imply that the job isn't serious. It's a very serious job, but it is in no way an "office job."

The singular advantage of being a flight attendant is that you have a lot of spare time for doing the things that you like to do. Do you love to go skiing? You can camp out in Vail all winter. Are you a dedicated diver? You can commute up from Cozumel, if you want to.

It's a lucrative profession—and you can combine it with other professions. You can be a real estate broker or a lawyer or a design consultant. You can meet many people. You can become a seasoned world traveler. And, if worse comes to worst, you can even marry an airline pilot.

There's a reason, of course, why we pilots choose flight attendants. We flirt with the Earthlings. We may even fall in love with some of them. But when push comes to shove, we'll often marry a flight attendant. We know that, in real life, we need a spouse who understands airline problems.

My own Mrs. X, who used to be a flight attendant, and who has a pretty good idea what it's like to fly airplanes nowadays, has kindly consented to give a few opinions to us. I'll pass them along, trying my best not to make comments on them.

"My husband" (she says) "is a typical airplane pilot. He's an overgrown kid. His planes are the toys he plays with. When you live with a pilot, that's something you get used to. It's the curse of these guys—but it's what keeps up their energy levels.

"Life with a pilot is one of feast versus famine. They're either off somewhere flying, or else they're around causing trouble for you. It's like living with a retiree. You think, Why doesn't he get out of here? Then suddenly he's gone, and you say, 'When is he coming home again?'

"Unlike those women who depend on their husbands ('Could you talk to our lawyer?' 'Could you please spank our son this evening?'), the wife of a pilot has to learn self-sufficiency. When a problem comes up, she has to handle it like a single woman. The joke in our family is that my husband is 'The Phantom.' Some of our friends think that our children are fatherless. Even my mother says she suspects I just rented him. She says I paid him five dollars to say 'I do' at the wedding ceremony.

"The thing about my husband is that his moods are so cyclical. He'll appear at the door. I haven't seen him for weeks now. Suddenly he's home, and it's like being on a honeymoon. We'll spend hours in bed. We'll spend days catching up with each other.

"But then, after a while, I start noticing the symptoms. I'll look in my cupboard. All my cans have become alphabetized. When I open the freezer, all the fruit juice is color-coded. I watch him get antsy. I can see the time weighing on him.

"Then off he goes again—and I'm left with PTA meetings. I shortcut the laundry. I cheat on my kitchen duty. During the days he was home we had pot roasts and veal dishes. Now the children and I will have Domino's Pizza orgies. It's a crazy kind of life, but it's the life that I'm used to. It's the life our friends lead. It's the life of all airline people. And as for terrorists and thunderstorms and microbursts and takeoff crashes, I'm used to those worries. Over the years, I've become hardened to them."

So speaks my wife—and with a fair amount of accuracy, probably. Of course I tend to be biased—she's the best thing that's happened to me. But I have to admit, our profession is divorce-ridden, and, since deregulation, there's been an explosion of family problems.

According to a university study that was done on three airline companies—two of them "stable," one with financial problems—emotionally stressed workers show a plethora of health concerns. Fully 21 percent of pilots at the "unstable" line had had a psychiatric illness recently.

At the more stable lines, the picture looked "average." Fewer than one in ten pilots had been denied a recent job promotion. That's in contradistinction to the unstable airline, where more than one in five pilots had gone ten years without a rank advancement.

When spouses were questioned, the statistics grew shocking. At the unstable line, 40 percent of wives had depressive symptoms. One in three families had high-to-severe marital stress, and a whopping 75 percent said that they were suffering from "economic pressures." At the healthier lines, it wasn't so nightmarish. Only one in twelve pilots had been to visit a psychiatrist lately. That may not be good, but it's better than at the unstable line, where more than one in four pilots were being treated just for depressive symptoms.

So now you know why we say our skies are less "friendly" nowadays. During the happiest times we have too many drinking problems. According to that study, at the "unstable" airline, *fully 13 percent of pilots admitted to hitting the bottle heavily.*

Now I've heard Frank Lorenzo. I'm familiar with his party line. He says that airlines like Eastern don't have any safety problems. I'm glad to hear that. I'd have been a bit worried otherwise. See, I happen to know that it was Eastern that was that "unstable" airline company.

# Chapter 13

# Of Statistics and Politics

Flying a plane is a complicated enterprise. It's mechanical, it's technical—and, as we saw, it can get personal sometimes. It's also something else. It can also be political. For the next several pages, I'd like to look at how those lines are drawn.

When deregulation first started, everyone was for it. Conservatives were for it because it would help slash big government. Liberals were for it because it coincided with the consumer movement. The workingman was for it because it would provide him with a fare bonanza.

The original bill, which was authored by Ted Kennedy and coauthored by Howard Cannon, a senator from Nevada, was signed by Jimmy Carter in a climate of righteousness: Freddie Laker was a hero, and the airlines were seen as gouging everybody. The bill's main provisions were to (1) do away with price restrictions; (2) open markets to all domestic carriers; (3) allow buyouts and mergers of route structures; and (4) eliminate the Civil Aeronautics Board, which at the time was the regulatory arm.

It didn't take long before the problems started surfacing. Small, local lines began to race to grab market shares. Cities were abandoned as being inconvenient or unprofitable. People were either stranded, or else forced to fly commuter services.

As the sins began multiplying we had an increase in "pilot errors." We had documented evidence of maintenance and training shortcuts. We had skyrocketing delays, we had mushrooming baggage snafus. And we had alarming "near-misses," not to mention less passenger comfort.

One's view of these issues tends to depend upon one's prejudices. Every major newspaper has taken an "editorial position" on it. They've buttressed their positions by rolling out "statistical evidence." They've thrown around numbers like some of our handlers throw the luggage you give them.

The problem with numbers is that they aren't always trustworthy. Do you want to prove safety? You can prove that flying is safer nowadays. You simply pull out figures for the 1978–86 accident fatalities. You'll see a decline in air crashes, and you can credit deregulation for that.

Do you want to prove danger? You can also prove the danger thesis. You can trot out statistics for the year 1987. In 1987 we had a very bad accident year, so you can use that to prove that deregulation is slaughtering everybody.

Reader, beware. All such "facts" are manipulatable. We are dealing in an area of negligible accident data. One major accident can make a year seem disastrous. It doesn't prove a thing about the state of the airline industry.

Everyone I know has his own personal ax to grind. If you're pro-deregulation you can point to lower ticket fares. You can show that poor working people are traveling more often and are paying significantly less money than they did back in the regulated era. If you're antideregulation you can show that that's delusional. You can show that full-fare prices are quintuple what they used to be. Even discounted fares, which are becoming less "discounted," are mostly the result of bigger planes and lower jet fuel prices.

The statistical game extends to just about everything. How often have you heard that flying is the safest means of passenger travel? The method for proving this is inevitably "passenger miles"—that is, the number of passengers multiplied by the number of miles they've covered. If, instead of using miles, you decide to base it on *time* spent traveling, then getting there by plane is not the sure thing it seems to be. More people get killed on our roads than in our skyways, but that's because the average U.S. traveler spends relatively little time in an airplane body.

Perhaps the silliest statistics are our vaunted "on time" statistics. The Department of Transportation has used these as political bludgeons. They have been publishing statistics of lines' relative arrival data, with the clear implication that if you're late you must be guilty of something. The trouble with that is that arrivals are a scheduling game. All an airline has to do is change its published arrival times. The planes will be punctual—but they won't have moved the passengers faster. In fact, they may have moved them slower. They won't have held for late-connecting passengers.

My own particular prejudice is that I happen to have to *fly* this equipment. I see things from the perspective not of numbers, but of the strain I'm feeling. Listed below are some of our current points of controversy. I'm going to try to define them, not with figures, but in terms of the angst they're causing.

## The Labor Controversy

You'll sometimes hear it said, "Aw, the problem is those union people. Deregulation would work if it weren't for those labor agitators." There's a certain amount of confusion over the role of the unions and whether, as Frank Lorenzo says, all we're hearing is labor propaganda.

The first thing to know is that not all airlines are unionized. Some have no unions. Some are swimming in union contracts. One of Lorenzo's big problems is that he has a contract with his mechanics that pays up to $80,000 a year for one man to handle your baggage for you!

Some nonunion workers are doing better than the unionized ones. Strangled by contracts, many companies grew desperate. They went to their unions and said, "Look, show us mercy or we'll shut these hubs down and there won't be any more jobs for anybody." The result of this squeeze is what is known as the "B scale." "B scale" employees work for greatly reduced pay packages. They do the same kind of work as their counterparts, the "A scalers," but they may have no guarantee that they will ever achieve pay parity with them.

You may think of all this as being irrelevant to your travel problems. Actually it isn't—it can have a very direct impact on you. When you're standing in line and trying to deal with a ticket agent, that agent, being a "B scaler," may be less competent than the old-style agent.

The "B scale" employees come from a very different applicant pool. They may be less educated. They may not speak English fluently. They're holding a job that's paying barely over minimum and perhaps only a little more than half of what the agent who preceded them was making.

From the *agents'* point of view, they're getting an incredibly tense work environment. They went with the airline because it seemed better than the

Burger King. Now they're confronted with more hostile people than they'd face in a year of working as a cell guard in Soledad.

The unions, of course, are extraordinarily frustrated. They've got their old-line employees whom they are trying to keep protected, but they've got all these new people who aren't reaping any benefits, and if they try to intercede they're faced with layoffs and bankruptcy proceedings.

This has naturally resulted in some very poor work relationships. The least little incident can touch off a labor conflict. Add a couple of hard-noses like Carl Icahn and Frank Lorenzo, and it's virtually inevitable that there are going to be knife fights and blood lettings.

A famous example of our down-and-dirty labor practices was the publicized case of Elizabeth Rich, a TWA attendant. A twenty-four-year employee, Rich was flying to Paris when she tried to smuggle milk out of an L-1011 passenger cabin. As she got off the plane, she was approached by a supervisor. Her belongings were searched and they found the four purloined milk cartons. In accordance with the rules, she was immediately "terminated." Her quarter-century service didn't serve as any advantage for her.

Now I'm not about sit here and defend recidivistic milk smugglers, but what makes this small case so politically significant is that Rich, who had been active in the struggle against Carl Icahn (TWA's board chairman), was an "A scale" employee, whereas her replacement was a "B scaler." The reason she was searched was because of a "tip" from a coworker. The coworker and Rich had had a dispute over an apartment lease. It would all work out perfectly, both for the coworker and for the airline: the coworker would get the apartment and the airline would get a cheap labor replacement.

As of the time of this writing, this case still hasn't been settled yet. The out-of-work Rich gained the ear of some television journalists. As she stated on "60 Minutes," while she admits to the milk theft, she is reasonably convinced that she was fired for her union activities. The airline, of course, denies all such villainy. "A theft is a theft" is how TWA looks at it. They'll admit to the fact that they were responding to a tipster, but it was Rich who did wrong, and all they did was take advantage of it.

It's this kind of thing that's been poisoning the atmosphere. There was an Eastern Airlines mechanic who had a run-in with his supervisor. He had discovered a bad floorplate in a DC-9 passenger cabin, and when he delayed the flight to fix it he was threatened with job dismissal. Indeed, the workers at Texas Air are constantly walking on eggshells. They have been notified by management that they are allowed five "occurrences." Any sixth "occurrence"—including a one-minute tardiness—will mean that they're fired. And it doesn't make any difference how long they've been working there.

The inevitable result is that workers have learned to protect themselves. There have been pilots at some airlines who have been threatened with job dismissal. The casebooks are filled with literally hundreds of instances in which pilots have been excoriated for claiming that their airplanes lacked "airworthiness." At some hardpressed airlines, it's almost a combat zone. There have been instances of arson. There have been cases of vandalism. There have cases of crew members who have flown while incapacitated, but who have begged not to be "squealed" on, because they didn't have any sick time left.

I should make it quite clear that not all the lines work this way. Indeed, my line does not. Neither do the other good ones. But we have a troubled "bottom group" that is hurting the industry, and the anxiety they've caused has affected almost everybody.

## The ALPA Connection

Among the various unions which engage in tough labor struggles is a group based in Washington called the Airline Pilots Association (ALPA). "Al-pa," as it's pronounced, was founded in the thirties and represents some forty-one thousand pilots who are employed by forty-six airline companies.

In ways that I think are not generally appreciated, ALPA is a protector of people who buy airplane tickets. They are a very vocal advocate of safety and operating standards, and if you didn't have ALPA you'd almost have to invent an equivalent for them.

When you get on an airplane you'll see an example of ALPA's safety program. There's a little plastic plaque that's on the back of each passenger seat. It will remind you of the fact that you should always keep your seat belt buckled, because even in smooth flight you can hit windshear and air turbulence.

That simple little tag represents several years of ALPA struggle. The airlines didn't want it because they were afraid that it would frighten people. ALPA took the position that people weren't that skittish and that they needed to be reminded that they weren't sitting at home in their living rooms somewhere.

The worth of this struggle was amply illustrated on an April afternoon back in 1988. That's when an Aloha Airlines jet, on its way to Honolulu, ruptured in flight and lost about a third of its fuselage covering. Of the ninety-two people in the back of that airplane, only one had the misfortune of being swept from the passenger cabin. That was a female flight attendant who was standing in the aisle at the time. All the others were safe— they had paid attention to those seat belt warnings.

When an accident takes place, ALPA will often investigate it. They'll churn through the wreckage with the NTSB and the FAA inspectors. They're one of the primary forces in getting to the heart of an incident and making sure things don't get buried under the inevitable "pilot error" carpet.

I'm not in agreement with all ALPA principles (I should mention that some airlines have their own independent unions), but I definitely think pilots need union representation, and in an imperfect world I applaud the integrity they've shown.

## The Security Controversy

The same can't be said for the Department of Transportation. Here we have examples of political appointeeism. On too many occasions, they've gone the way that the wind is blowing. They'll announce silly rules, then end up having to retract them again.

For instance:

It was 1987. The place was California. A disgruntled ex-employee for the USAir company managed to smuggle a gun aboard a PSA airliner, shoot the two pilots, and send the plane into a mountainside. In the wake of this incident, DOT was beside itself. They immediately ordered frisks of all the flight crews and flight attendants. Pilots and stewardesses were expected to line up with passengers; all flights would be delayed while we passed through the metal detectors.

Let us grant for a moment that there is a need for tighter security measures. An employee with a grudge can do an incalculable amount of airplane damage. Nobody knows better than a veteran airline pilot how easy it is to foil some airports' security systems.

Nevertheless, this was an inappropriate political move. Frisking a pilot is like frisking a brain surgeon. What are you going to do, tell him he shouldn't have sharp objects on him? If I wanted to harm my passengers, I certainly wouldn't need a gun to do it.

The "rights" of the citizen are often left at the passenger gate. We willingly submit to all kinds of indignities. We do so with the knowledge that being trapped in an airplane is a special situation which we are willing to make compromises for. The problem for pilots is that we *live* in that environment. We are willing to accept that we have grave responsibilities; but to penalize us all because of one madman's actions is about like penalizing the police because a cop accidentally shot somebody.

## The Drug and Alcohol Challenge

One of the hottest union battles as we head into the nineties is in reaction to proposals for random drug testing. To appreciate this problem, we have to look at yet another problem. We have to look at what's been done about drunkenness and alcoholism.

Back in the early 1970s, when I first got my captain's stripes, I had a youngish first officer who had a very bad drinking problem. One cold winter's day we were heading for the airport and this guy was so hung over he began to vomit out the limousine window.

We pulled the car over. I said, "Listen, you idiot. This is a Christmas Eve flight. We don't have any other pilots available. I'm going to take you to Chicago, but after that I'm replacing you. Our line can't afford to leave a planeload of people stranded."

The guy started grousing. "I can make it," he told me.

"You don't understand. We'll have a half-dozen flight attendants watching us. If they turn your ass in, you're going to be through in this industry. You're going to lose your pilot's license, and they'll nail me for trying to cover for you."

We got on the plane. I flew him to Chicago. Fortunately for me, we didn't have any emergencies that day. When we got to O'Hare I led him to the crew desk and I said, "Here—this guy's sick. You'll have to get me a replacement for him."

This was typical of the way we used to handle pilots' drinking problems. It was lax and it was crude. I look back and I cringe at it. If a pilot had a problem, all the other pilots covered for him. It was an unwritten rule, and it had the complicity of the airline companies.

The past fifteen years have seen a remarkable turnaround. We have cleaned up our act. We have rules, and we observe those rules. In fact, I believe I can safely say that there is no other industry whose practitioners are held to such a high degree of professionalism.

Consider:

*A pilot can't drink in the hours before flight time.* These hours may vary. It depends on the line you fly for. The minimum curfews are from eight to twelve hours, but there are still several airlines that demand a full twenty-four-hour "bottle-to-throttle" period.

*We are proscribed from flying while taking medications.* Because of our more stressful scheduling, pilots may be tempted to ignore head colds. Dristan and Contac cause dizziness and drowsiness. We pilots are warned, and we can be in trouble if we ignore those warnings.

*We are cautioned against flying even with untreated sinus conditions.* A block of the eustachians can cause dizziness and balance problems. Unfortunately, colds are an occupational hazard, and the flight pay we lose can occasionally be considerable.

*Drug tests aside, we already have physical exams.* A major airline pilot is a laboratory guinea pig. As a captain, I'm subjected to two semiannual physicals—and, yes, during those physicals I have to turn in some urine samples.

Nevertheless—

In 1988, the Secretary of Transportation, a man named James Burnley, ordered random drug testing for all transportation workers—including commercial airline pilots, many of whom got angry about it.

To understand why you have to understand us airline pilots. We are not the kinds of guys to find our pleasure in a drug ampule. God knows we may drink—drinking is almost a ritual with us—but we are a very different breed from your average bus driver or Amtrak worker. There was a study at American that helps to support this assertion. They gave standard drug tests to all of American's new job applicants. Among the nonpilot applicants, they had the usual number of positives. In a country like ours, that can run up to 20 percent of applicants nowadays.

But among new pilot applicants, there were fewer than *1 percent.* That's a 1-percent figure for guys who haven't even been interviewed yet. And since drug testing new applicants is now standard at all airlines, you can feel relatively sure that that 1 percent never makes it to simulator training.

Of course it would be silly to say that no pilot was ever a drug user. Pilots my age came out of the wild 1960s. I've known plenty of guys who have smoked marijuana cigarettes or eaten hashish-laced brownies that were given to them at a party at some point. But it's not "what we do." We are an extremely square social order. Few of us smoke; most of us are concerned about our cholesterol intake. If one of our cohorts starts to act irresponsibly, you can believe me it's noted—and you can be sure that proper steps are taken.

When someone first proposed that I ought to sit down and write this book, he gave me a suggestion as to what the first line should be. He said that a zingy first line would be, "My copilot was drunk—again." He said, "It's that kind of thing that will make it hit the best-seller lists."

You will be gratified to note that that is not the first line we used. I refuse to be party to that kind of sensationalism. If you want to read stories about wild men and drug abusers, buy a supermarket tabloid. They'll even throw in some UFOs for you.

Perhaps a more serious story concerns drug use among our controller force. There have been several air traffic controllers who have admitted to cocaine abuse. I can appreciate the dilemma that Jim Burnley is confronting since, in order to weed out those people, he has to deal with all of us other transportation workers.

But if there is no other message you take away from this story, I hope I can convince you that we pilots are responsible. If a pilot acts up, he becomes the scourge of the industry. No one will fly with him. He gets drummed from the fraternal order.

That notwithstanding, drugs are obviously a problem nowadays. Our government is concerned about just who's sitting in that cockpit up there. To address these concerns, the solution it's come up with is that we should unzip our pants and randomly pee in a urinalysis bottle.

And as of November 1988, that's exactly what we've been doing.

But this Draconian solution is a little like that frisk proposal. There had been a precipitating accident which had aroused the political hackles. An Amtrak worker had caused a very serious train derailment, and when it was learned that he was on drugs it created nationwide newspaper headlines. Elizabeth Hansford Dole, who was Jim Burnley's predecessor, reacted by asking for drug tests for everybody. She did this precipitously, without consulting with the union people, and as a result many pilots began to feel that their rights were violated.

As to whether that's true, I'll leave that to the legal scholars. As of the time of this writing, it's still dragging through the court system. But what I *can* say for sure is that random drug testing runs counter to the philosophy that we've established with our alcohol program.

The pilots' alcohol program is the envy of the transport world. I can speak on this subject, because I've had a fair amount of experience with it.

Back in the mid-1970s, shortly after that copilot fiasco, I became involved with this program and was one of the more active participants in it.

The program is called HIMS. That's short for Human Intervention and Motivation Systems. It was pushed by various unions, and there was a lot of resistance to it. There were an awful lot of pilots who wanted to deny that there was a drinking problem, and it took many long years before the industry became accommodated to it.

The idea behind HIMS is to unearth your substance abusers. You do this through reason and through an appeal to their pragmatism. You say, "You've got a good future. You can continue to pursue it. But you're not going to fly until you've cleaned up your drinking problem."

Prior to HIMS, we had an entirely different approach to things. If you "ratted" on a buddy, that buddy was terminated. Many worried wives watched their husbands get pickled and were afraid to speak up because there wouldn't be any food on the table. After HIMS came along, there was a complete change of atmosphere. Now known problem drinkers were confronted by their coworkers. They were told, "Look, pal, get help. Nobody's going to fire you, but if you don't take the cure, you're never going to sit at those controls again."

This program isn't easy. There can be a lot of resentment over it. For one thing, of course, the pilot still has his license lifted. He may have been spared the indignity of firing, but there are FAA rules, and those rules require no flying privileges.

He'll also spend years having to undergo a rehab program. He'll be constantly monitored by professionals and trained coworkers. He can fly when he's treated, but he'll still be subject to spot urine tests. A person who's been an abuser has to surrender certain privacy privileges.

A program like this is so much better than a drug test program. It ameliorates guilt. It doesn't drive people underground. It helps preserve a relationship of trust and mutuality, which is so terribly important within the confines of a flight compartment.

I am very much aware that, should we have one big drug-related air crash, all reason and subtlety will be thrown out the window. But until that day comes, I'm against random drug tests. We can achieve the same ends more justly by extending the HIMS program.

# The FAA Wrangle

As a pilot, I don't claim to be an expert on Washington. Bureaucracy and I don't get along terribly well together. I'm certainly not an expert on the Federal Aviation Administration, except as it happens to affect me and my plane and what my controller says to me.

Nevertheless, this is becoming a bone of contention nowadays. Critics are saying that the FAA should be overhauled. *The Wall Street Journal*, which takes an interest in such matters, has gone so far as to say that it should go the way of the AT&T monopoly.

First, let's review what the FAA is responsible for. It establishes rules for training and flight safety. It maintains our towers. It has certain law enforcement privileges. It can take away licenses, and it can even ground whole airline companies.

Since the Johnson administration, back in the flush 1960s, the FAA has been part of the Department of Transportation. That makes it no different from Amtrak or the St. Lawrence Seaway project. It also makes it vulnerable to politics and committee bickering.

A few years ago, at United Airlines, they decided that Dulles would make an ideal hub facility. They announced their intentions in about the middle of the winter, and some six months later they began flying their equipment in there.

The FAA went to the Department of Transportation. They said, "Hey, listen, guys, we're going to get traffic into Dulles suddenly. We need more controllers. We need a whole lot more hardware out there. We don't have enough lights, and we don't have enough ramp facilities."

The DOT's reaction, at least as I heard it, was to say, "Okay, no problem. Just send us a memo on it. In a couple of months we'll get a committee to study it. In about a year and a half we'll have a few more controllers for you."

Well, hell.

I mean, you can't run this business on the metabolism of a post office employee. Airplanes are fast. So are the people who work with airplanes. You can't hold up traffic while you sit in a committee counting the number of paper clips you'll need to put in a new facility somewhere.

The Department of Transportation is a big, fat bureaucracy. It is often a sinecure for winners of the spoils system. Our lean airline business needs to be free and independent. You can't plan your moves when you've got a thousand tons of committee work sitting on you.

138

There was a true-to-life story that helps to illustrate the politics angle. It was late in the summer of 1988. Michael Dukakis was scheduled to make a campaign speech, only his airplane got grounded because of an unannounced FAA inspection.

The Democrats were furious. They burned up the telephone lines. They proclaimed this a foul—it was dirty-tricks Republicanism. After all, the FAA was part of the Department of Transportation, and the Department of Transportation was a hotbed of Reagan appointees.

That poor FAA guy went through agony defending himself. What to him was a duty was to them a political maneuver. All he had wanted to do was to assure that the plane was safe. He precipitated a tempest that threatened to rival the Watergate break-in.

The acidity involved can get pretty incredible sometimes. There was an FAA inspector who got suspicious of some Boeing operations. He began making certain noises about the 737 and what appeared to be a flaw and a possible suppression of some simulator information.

One night, in his motel, he was awakened by a phone call.

"Jim Marquis?" said the caller. (That happened to be who the inspector was.) "This is Senator Henry Jackson. Do you know who I am? I'm the senator from Washington. I want to know why you're persecuting us."

The gist of this call was that Marquis should lay off the Boeing people. Boeing, in Seattle, is a major economic center. Should the news have gotten around that the Seven-Three had mechanical problems, the company could suffer. That could lead to serious labor layoffs.

It's this kind of thing that makes the FAA vulnerable. They regulate the industry, and they have a great deal of power over it; but at the same time they're governed by a political apparatus that owes its very existence to whomever is pulling the strings at the time.

To scrap the FAA would be highly irresponsible. It would be worse than what we went through with the breakup of the telephone company. The FAA, which runs our air traffic control system, is a complicated network, and it has a lot of little pieces connected to it.

To give you one example: The FAA works closely with our military. Some controllers have clearance to watch over Air Force and Navy maneuvers. For the military to be placed at the mercy of private industry would not only be inefficient, it would be dangerous to our defense commitments.

It might be possible to accomplish a few more modest objectives. We might at least make the FAA its own separate agency. We might give its administrator an independent tenure so that he wouldn't have to leave every time the political winds started changing. We had a chat with one official, and he put it succinctly to us: "We all have to suffer no matter who wins at election time. Whoever's in the White House, it means a whole new bureaucracy for us. And since they're all new to flying, we have to waste hundreds of hours explaining things to them."

These are some of the questions that our Congress should wrestle with. I suspect they soon will—there have been just too many criticisms recently. But I hope, when they do, they use subtlety and delicacy. Let's not repeat all the errors that were committed when deregulation was enacted.

# Chapter 14

# The Educated Flier

Up to now I've been critical of the people in my industry. I've been critical of myself. I've been critical of the politicians we deal with. I've also been critical of some of our less desirable airline passengers. I'd like to take this opportunity to make sure that you don't become one of them.

Too many people just don't bother to inform themselves. They simply show up. They say, "Here I am, take me somewhere." For the next several pages I'd like to lead you through a plane trip and, at the risk of sounding stuffy, make an "educated flier" out of you.

## How to Buy an Airline Ticket

Buying a ticket isn't what it was fifteen years ago. Before deregulation, you just went into an airline office. If there was an opening, they'd tell you. If there wasn't, they'd tell you. It was all cut and dried—and they'd even book you on a competitor's airline.

In 1989, if you want to buy an airplane ticket, going to the airline may be the worst way of doing it. Not only may you end up paying more than you need to, you may be told there are no seats when actually there are plenty of seats available.

There's a little-known entity called a "packager" or "consolidator." A consolidator is a middleman who buys up large blocks of airline seats. He'll resell those seats to your local retail travel agent, who will sell them to you, taking a healthy little commission out of it.

Most airline companies don't work through consolidators. If a consolidator buys a seat, to the company that seat is "occupied." It has no way of knowing that the seat is still available. That can only be determined by going through your local retail travel agent.

When you go to a travel agent, don't just take the first flight he offers. Travel agents use computers that are tied to reservations services. These sophisticated services are divisions of major airlines, and they are inevitably programmed to promote that particular lines' flight schedules.

Make sure that your agent keeps scrolling through his computer files. Often, "through" flights (that is, flights that involve connecting flights) are considerably cheaper than nonstop flights. Schedules keep changing. Make sure he keeps your options open. A flight that's full today may next week have ten seats available.

Given the enormous disparity that exists between fares nowadays—one airline's fare may cost three times what another is offering—the amount that you save can be very considerable. And you may also end up getting a somewhat more desirable airline out of it.

## Preconfirmed Seat Assignments

I am continually amazed, when I walk through an airport terminal, that there are always hoards of people who are standing at the ticket counters. They'll have shown up early—which is an excellent idea nowadays—but they'll have never taken the time to arrange for a preconfirmed seat assignment.

You can get this assignment by simply requesting it from your travel agent. You can also call the airline up to twenty-four hours before flight time. Once you've got your seat, that will avoid most of the other problems. If you don't have your seat, then some of the following might happen to you:

# The Smoking vs. Nonsmoking Hassle

"Will that be smoking or nonsmoking?"

"I'd prefer to have nonsmoking."

The ticket agent scowls. She hits some keys on her computer keyboard. "I'm sorry," she says. "Our nonsmoking's filled right now. I'll put you in smoking, and you can take it up with the flight attendant."

Hold on. Stop right there. You are now on a collision course. A nonsmoking passenger cannot be forced to sit in the smoking section. It may be true, as she says, that you'll have to talk to a flight attendant, but if the nonsmoking section is filled, they'll have to convert a row in the smoking area.

The same can't be said of smokers in a nonsmoking section. People who smoke have to give way to the nonsmokers. It's amazing to me that not all flight attendants know this. You'll still see confusion right up to the moment they're sealing the airplane exits.

The way the law reads, if you're flying domestically, smoking is prohibited on flights of two hours or less. That's two hours *scheduled.* If the flight extends longer, you still can't light up. You've got to go by the *scheduled* flight time.

The same does not apply for all the overseas carriers. Our European brethren are notably behind in their smoking mores. You'll still see some lines that put their smokers amidships, or—what confounds some Americans—along one side of the airplane body.

Let me say about smoking that, although I gave it up years ago, it's the nonsmokers nowadays who are causing most of the headaches for us. They've become so evangelical that it's worth your life dealing with them. They've got God on their side. All we've got is the FAA manual.

Interestingly, smoking had at least one minor advantage going for it. It helped our inspectors when they were checking for metal fatigue. They'd look at the seams. If they saw seams with brown tar streaks coming from them, they knew they were bad; it meant that there was a leak from the passenger cabin.

In 1988, to the dismay of R. J. Reynolds, the people at Northwest scrapped their domestic flights' smoking sections. They did this, they said, as strictly a "good-will social gesture," but it could also have been justified from a dollars-and-cents perspective.

For one thing, of course, smoking is hard on the flight attendants. Unlike the passengers, our attendants remain ambulatory. They are up and about and in a very dry air environment. The smoke near the ceiling creates a very real health hazard for them.

But there's another thing, too: Take a look at an airliner body. In the back, near the tail, you'll see a hole with a streak coming out of it. That's a nicotine streak. That's what you're breathing in the passenger cabin. It costs millions of dollars in added maintenance and housekeeping expenditures.

The wave of the future is undoubtedly with the nonsmokers. Even some European carriers are beginning to reexamine their smoking policies. It's a fairly safe bet that within the next couple of years you'll find that all the major lines have followed the lead of the Northwest people.

## Carry-ons vs. Checked Luggage

Since deregulation, we've had numerous baggage problems. The expansion of routes made for inadequate ramp facilities. We've had instances of lines gaining a hold in an airport and bringing in planes even when they didn't have any baggage trucks to serve them.

Many "smart" travelers have taken to relying on carry-ons. Nothing wrong with that—it saves waiting for your baggage later. The only problem is, how do you define what's a "carry-on"? "If I can carry it, it's on," is the way some people seem to be looking at it.

A story is told about a flight out of Kennedy. There were some Puerto Rican travelers who had a very heavy garment bag with them. They asked the flight attendant to hang it up in the closet section. The bag was so heavy she couldn't get it onto the hook provided.

Becoming suspicious, she looked in the garment bag. There, to her horror, was the body of a dead woman. It was one of their grandmothers. She had died in Manhattan, and they were trying to get her back without having to pay an extra airfare for her.

Now I won't accuse you of trying to take your dead grandmother with you, but I'll remind you of the fact that you're restricted to two carry-ons. The allowable size is up to the line and its flight crew, but one bag must be such that it can slide under a nine-inch-high airplane seat.

In the event of lost luggage, you should be properly compensated. At present, the limit is $1,250. Each major line has its own peculiar restrictions, so report your loss immediately and be sure to follow the instructions they give you.

# The Overbooking Blues

Sometimes you'll arrive to find that there aren't *any* seats available. They've overbooked your flight. They'll ask you to go and stand in a corner somewhere. Now you'll have to survive what seems to be the equivalent of a game show episode. If you agree not to fly, they'll offer you a fabulous prize of some sort.

Understand this: Most lines' flights are overbooked nowadays. Each major line uses computerized reservations systems. They know from experience that there will be a certain number of "no shows," and they factor that in when they're figuring their flight reservations.

This was no problem back when the lines were still regulated. Back then, if they erred, they'd just bring another airplane in there. It was not that unheard of to be on an L-1011 and have so many empty seats you felt like you were alone in a football stadium.

I know that was nice, but try to look at it from our side. This business I'm in has an extremely slim profit margin. As a matter of fact, it's about 1.5 percent, which puts it second in slimness only to your neighborhood supermarket. On a typical flight, let's say there are three empty coach seats back there. Those three empty seats can be that entire plane flight's profit margin. We'll do anything we can to try to put some warm bodies in there. That may inconvenience you, but for us it's a survival issue.

In domestic air travel, we have minimal overbooking problems. It's been figured so finely that there are relatively few compensations given. There had better not be many—overbooking is expensive. It costs an airline a fortune to give those free trips and bonuses to people.

Travel abroad can get a little more hair-raising. I've heard some pretty nasty stories about European air carriers. I heard a story about one line where they locked passengers in the lavatories and took off with flight attendants sitting in people's laps and in the cabin aisles.

To foil overbooking, try to get there ahead of time. A half-hour is minimum if you're traveling domestically. If you're traveling abroad, I would recommend two hours—and particularly if the line is not one of the major industrial country carriers.

# The "No-Show" Problem

One reason, of course, that we have overbooking is that there are some very clever people who reserve seats and then don't show up for them. This has been a major pain in the neck for every U.S. and European air carrier, and we've been all too tardy in taking steps to eradicate it.

A typical case will be the egotistical business traveler. He'll intercom his secretary: "Book me a ticket to Chicago, Mary." Only one's not enough. He'll decide he needs five tickets. He has some meetings to attend, and he's not sure when they'll be over exactly.

Well, God bless his hide, he's creating havoc throughout the airline industry. Because he travels so much, we've bent over backward to accommodate him. But he's abusing the privilege. He's clogging the system, and he's denying other passengers their right to get a plane reservation.

Within the past year or two, we've taken steps to correct this problem. We've got computers nowadays that are pretty good at combing passenger lists. When they turn up a name that's on a duplicate passenger list, an alarm bell goes off, and that guy gets a call from the reservations department.

Some lines will tell him what flight he's going to take whether he likes it or not, and others will just cancel all his reservations. It depends on the line and how generous it feels.

So my message to you is, *One to a customer.* You're contributing to the chaos, and you're not really gaining anything. Take a few minutes to try to nail down your schedule better. And if your meeting gets out early, go and sign up as a "standby" passenger.

# The Mediocre Meal Problem

Airline meals will never be restaurant meals. A restaurant, at most, may cook for several hundred dinner patrons. An airline's flight kitchen cooks for tens of thousands of dinner patrons, and the food has to be refrigerated and then warmed up in a warming oven.

There is an alternative. When you enter a flight kitchen, you'll see a food assembly plant that practically rivals a car factory. Conveyors of chops are continually dumped into vast meat bins, where hair-netted women slap them quickly into tray compartments.

It's a little unappetizing.

But in the back of that kitchen, perhaps off to the side somewhere, past the utensil-wrapping gadget and the slicers and the napkin folders, you'll see a small operation that's about the size of a restaurant kitchen in which trays are being assembled, individually, on serving dollies.

This is your place—it's where they make the "special diet menus." All the meals here are prepared individually. Whether kosher or salt-free or vegetarian or diabetic, they are handled in an atmosphere that rivals at least a pretty decent restaurant operation.

My advice to the traveler is to order from these special menus. It doesn't matter what—you can order salt-free, and then put salt on it. But if you order this food (you can do it at the time you buy your airline ticket), it will be better prepared, and there will be no extra charge for it.

## The Safety Dilemma

I'm always astonished, when flying on an airplane, to see how very few passengers pay attention to the safety reminders. They'll get on the plane, they'll plop down and start reading something, and they'll be totally oblivious, both to the plane and to the instructions given them.

An educated flier will always note where the exits are. He'll mentally compute the number of rows that are in his escape route. In the event of a fire, he'll be able to negotiate them. He'll "see" with his fingers and grope his way along the route he's calculated.

In connection with this, there have been suits by the handicapped. They're resentful of rules that forbid them from sitting in certain airline seats. Specifically, they object to what is often airline policy, that only able-bodied passengers be allowed to sit next to emergency exits.

With all due respect, I have to agree with the airlines here. Those doors weigh a ton. Their mechanisms are complicated. You can't allow people who can't see or who are incapacitated to bar other people from making their way to an emergency exit.

I might also suggest that you should pay attention to those evacuation instructions. They may seem perfunctory, but there is a very definite purpose for them. Perhaps you'll see why if we take a few minutes and review what goes on during a "survivable" airplane accident.

# Understanding Crashes

There are obviously some crashes that you will not walk away from. That's an ugly fact of life, and there's nothing we can do about it. But there are many, many crashes where passengers do survive, and it's incumbent upon you to do your best to become one of them.

Your biggest threat to life may not be the crash, it may be being suffocated. An airplane's interior is a wonderland of chemicals. It contains more synthetic materials than any room you can imagine, and getting free from all that smoke may be the most immediate challenge confronting you.

There was a deadly example involving an Air Canada airliner. It was flying out of Dallas, and it was headed toward Toronto. When a fire began smoldering in one of its tourist-class lavatories, it was able to land, and it appeared that a tragedy had been averted.

But within seconds of landing, the fire became suffocating. People began choking. The air became poisonous. By the time they were able to complete evacuation, twenty-three people had had the very life snuffed out of them.

At the FAA Center near Atlantic City, New Jersey, where tests are being performed to set fire and toxicity standards, they show films of what happens during an interior airplane cabin fire. It's a fire they've set purposely inside a specially equipped Convair fuselage.

When the fire first ignites, the interior just sits there. Those wool-covered seats all have flame-retardant blockers built into them. The source of the fire is a huge bin of kerosene. The flames are intense, but those walls are quite fire-resistant.

As the temperature soars, you'll see more and more smoke emitted. It's coming from the seats. It's coming from the wall interiors. It clings to the ceiling. It becomes a blanket of poison up there. If you were standing up, breathing, you wouldn't have much of a life expectancy.

But even with that, the plane still looks inhabitable. The seats are intact. The roof hasn't ignited yet. If you could keep yourself low, and prevent yourself from being blinded, you could probably get out—assuming you knew where the exits were.

But then something happens. The air becomes volatile. In the course of five seconds, that chamber transforms itself. It changes from a room that is fairly survivable to a kiln that is not. You're suddenly staring into a blast furnace.

This point of transition is what the experts call a "flashover." A huge ball of flame suddenly appears near the cabin ceiling. It rolls through the plane like an expulsion from a flamethrower. The interior explodes, and suddenly there's nothing but whiteness surrounding you.

An airliner's crew has ninety seconds to evacuate you. That isn't much time. It's not enough time to get your effects in order. One of the most serious impediments to the evacuation of an airliner is that the passengers don't *move.* Or else they move, but they try to bring things with them.

If you have to crash-land, don't worry about your garment carriers. Forget your valises. There is nothing that important in them. If an airplane depressurizes, put the mask on yourself first. Your child can come later. It's important that the parent stay conscious.

Speaking of children: One of the deadliest errors is to think that your arms can take the place of a safety belt. An infant in arms is not adequately protected; in the event of a crash, your baby will become a projectile in there.

Always make sure that your child has a seat belt on. If the child is too small, check with your flight attendant. Follow her instructions during takeoffs and landings. Even a rough landing can pose a danger to an unbelted toddler.

If you're flying over water, pay attention to those life vest instructions. As pilots, we're trained. We've been instructed in ditching maneuvers. We'll try to come down landing in the direction that the waves are going and with the body of the plane inside a trough between the swell configurations. (Admittedly, this part makes some airline pilots skeptical. It's all well and good to have lectures on ditching, but the idea of crash-landing while making a study of wave patterns looks better in print than from the deck of a plane that's crashing.)

(Nevertheless, I promise, we'll do our best.)

A liner may float for from five to sixty minutes. You'll exit by the wings. You'll get in a raft, and you'll get out of there. In the event of survival, there will be a chain of command to follow. It will start with the captain and run down through the various flight crew members.

I am happy to report that I have never had to do this procedure. Neither, to my knowledge, have any of the guys that I work with. But as you set off toward land, carrying your machete and your snakebite kit, be assured that your airline has the utmost confidence in you.

# Choosing the Safest Seat

A few years ago, I was sitting in a safety class. It was boring as hell. We had this FAA technician talking to us. He kept reeling off numbers about metal fatigue and g-forces, and after a while it became clear that none of us had the faintest idea what he was talking about.

Finally, from the back, came a question from a flight engineer:

"When *you* get on a plane, where do you, yourself, sit?" he asked him.

The tekkie just stood there. He looked totally nonplussed by that. Apparently, in all those years, nobody had ever thought to ask him that.

The answer he gave has been confirmed by some other experts. I'll pass it along, and you can do what you want with it. It's one man's opinion—but it's a reasonably educated opinion. If you were to ask me the question, I'd have to defer to what this specialist told us:

The back of the plane is most removed from the wing area. It's the wings and the middle that will get the most structural tearing. Those are also the areas that contain the plane's fuel reserves. It seems logical to assume that that will probably be where a fire gets started.

When you get on a plane, you should try to sit in the tail section. Sit on the aisle. Try to sit near an emergency exit. Take a few seconds and go and check out the overheads. The last thing you need is to have some heavy, blunt object fall on you.

If you familiarize yourself with the construction of an airliner, you'll note that the rear of the cabin sits on top of the baggage compartment. When that hold is filled up, it's the equivalent of a honeycomb. The tightly packed baggage acts like so many shock absorbers.

The tail of the plane is usually the part of least impact. If a liner goes down, it's likely to hit with the nose first. When the tail hits the ground, it will probably hit in a dragging motion. This helps further ameliorate whatever else may be happening back there.

Of course, there have been many, many crashes where it was the tail that took the brunt of it. A rear-mounted engine may catch fire from having jet fuel sucked through it. Certain airplane models have exits in their tail sections that are impossible to deploy if the plane has had to make a belly-landing.

But, generally speaking, cast your lot with the tail section. The only trouble is, the tail is also the smoking section. So actuarially speaking, it's a kind of damned-either-way dilemma: do you want to die quick, or do you prefer the long, cancerous method?

# *Airports: Convenience vs. Safety*

In 1988, in an issue of *Money,* they ran a survey of readers rating various U.S. airports. When I looked at that survey, I shook my head in bewilderment. Their most popular airports were invariably pilots' most hated ones.

Their number-one airport was Washington National. Now Washington National is an airline pilot's nightmare. It's an obsolete field stuck on the edge of the Potomac, and I'm always dismayed that we have so many world leaders flying in there.

When you're flying into National, you're often coming in visually. You're following the Potomac. That's a winding, twisting river valley. You're banking and weaving, and at the same time descending, and if you stray to either side there can be some very serious trouble waiting for you.

On your right you've got Langley. That's the CIA headquarters. To the left is the White House. You've also got the State Department. In front of the airport, and practically blocking it, is the Pentagon Building and a couple of naval facilities.

All of these areas are off-limits to aircraft. Violate their space, they will slap a very hefty penalty on you. You will certainly catch flak from your chief pilot's office, and if they want to get rough, they might even take your license away from you.

A few years ago, to relieve National's congestion, they built a very nice airport out at Dulles International. Do the VIPs use it? No, they want to use National. If convenience is at stake, people will always sacrifice safety for it.

Another popular field is New York City's La Guardia. "La Garbage," as we call it, was actually built on a garbage dump. As the surrounding urban sprawl kept growing closer, more threatening, it became the most congested single field in the entire world of commercial airplane flying.

Landing at La Garbage is about like landing on a lily pad. It has two stubby runways. Naturally, they intersect. Three of the four approaches are coming in over water, and as you're about to touch down, you suddenly find you've got a *wall* in front of you.

This entire piece of land is being lost to an estuary. It's been sinking at the rate of about a half-inch a decade. The runways are built on top of old concrete pilings and are abutted by dikes to try to keep some of the water from swallowing them.

To the guy who doesn't know this, it can be absolutely mind-blowing. Not only is it tough in terms of traffic and radio congestion, but you can be about to set down on that parapeted runway, "stub your toe" against the wall, and end up landing with your feet in the air!

Which, by the way, has happened a few times.

Another of its drawbacks is that it's only a few miles from Kennedy Airport. This means that you often have to come in using alternate approach patterns. If the weather is bad, or if it's a time of high air traffic, these two fields together have to be considered as one big superairport.

Nevertheless, La Guardia is beloved by the airplane passengers. It's close to the city, so they save a little taxi fare. Twenty miles away they've got a big field at Newark, but do they want to use Newark? No, they'd rather use La Guardia, thank you.

One field, thank heavens, that wasn't on that survey was a field that I talked about back when we were climbing through "Indian Country." San Diego's Lindbergh is one of this country's worst airports, and it always amazes me that we haven't had a lot more disasters out there.

When you're coming into Lindbergh you're virtually sliding down a mountainside. The normal approach is completely blocked by a mountain range. To land on this strip and have enough space to stop on, you have to slide down the hill as if you were a tram car with wires attached to you.

That's not so bad—you can pretend you're a tram car—but (typically California) this hill has got developments on it. So as you're coming down the mountain you're looking in hotel rooms, and you're seeing waiters and diners and, sometimes, half-naked women staring at you.

When you get to the runway, you can't land where you'd normally land. You have to flare the plane sharply and keep flying down the centerline. You have to put the wheels down beyond what's called a "displaced threshold," then slam into reverse and lift your spoilers and put your wheel brakes on.

To take off from San Diego is about as tricky as getting landed on it. Since the above-mentioned mountains are so close to the runway, as soon as you're up you have to veer and take evasive action. If I had my way, I'd just eliminate it from our airline schedules.

In a recent pilot survey, when they were asked about airports, Los Angeles International topped most pilots' "least favorite" list. That's no surprise. It has the San Gabriel Mountains, it has a big, smoggy city, and it has 20 percent of all private airplane traffic. Nevertheless, I don't mind poor old LAX. Mexico City has considerably more problems attached to it. Not only is it smoggy, it's incredibly mountainous, and, because it's so high, you get greatly reduced engine performance.

Don't get me wrong: None of these fields are condemnable. They all meet the standards that are required for safe plane operations. But on a comparative basis, they are less than what they should be. Short of shutting them down, I'd like to see a reduction of traffic at all of them.

# Rating the Airlines

I am not about to tell you that certain airlines are hazardous. All the major lines are relatively safe and dependable. Even the commuters, although they don't match the majors, are generally reliable in terms of maintenance and pilot training.

But you should be aware that there are three kinds of airlines. There are the well-known "majors," which handle 90 percent of the passenger traffic; there are the lesser-known regionals, which carry about 30 million passengers annually; and there are the so-called "air taxis," which are usually unscheduled airlines.

The major brand carriers are called "Part 121 carriers." That refers to a section in the FAA regulation manual. Their governance is strict. They have to meet the highest safety standards. They have to have a lot of expensive equipment, and they have to have very thorough pilot training.

The regionals, or commuters, are called "Part 135 carriers." These are lines that use planes that have thirty or fewer passenger seats. Because they don't have the money, but are needed by their communities, they are not held to standards anywhere close to what the big lines are held to.

A recently published study by a leading travel magazine showed that you are ten times more likely to be in a crash on a commuter line. Between 1979 and 1985 these lines suffered 1.27 fatalities per million passengers, compared with .3 per million for major carriers. The reasons for that are both training- and equipment-related. A little Piper Navajo isn't built like a McDonnell Douglas is. Even a sophisticated plane, such as a Saab or a De Havilland, requires a level of training beyond what some of those little lines can offer pilot candidates.

The story gets worse when you look at the air taxi companies. Here you have flights that aren't even always published in a timetable. They'll hire out for charter. They'll run semiregular puddle jumpers. You're about as safe on some of these lines as you may be flying with your uncle somewhere.

And I'm assuming your uncle isn't too good a flier.

A documented account of a company called Provincetown-Boston Airlines (PBA) tells of how, on November 29, 1983, the owner of the company, a man named John van Arsdale, flew a planeload of passengers from Hyannis down to Jacksonville. About forty minutes out, they sprang a leak in their hydraulic fluid. This is the fluid that affects a plane's brakes and some of its flight controls. Van Arsdale kept flying. He didn't consider that serious. He flew clear down to Jacksonville, where he ordered another plane to meet them.

The plane they now boarded was called a Nihon YS-11. The Nihon YS-11 is a Japanese turboprop. They boarded this plane, and they flew it down to Naples. According to the log, it was one "Captain John R. Wales" who flew it.

The only trouble is, there was no Captain John R. Wales on board. Captain John R. Wales was a thousand miles away from there. The plane was actually flown by Van Arsdale and his copilot, neither one of whom had ever been trained to captain a YS-11.

I don't mean to imply that all small airlines are run that way. Most of them aren't. Most of them are competent. But our air taxi annals are chock full of horror stories. Be careful of these lines. You'd do well to check them out ahead of time.

Setting that aside, when you're flying with the majors, is there any reliable way for a passenger to make a judgment of them? I'm willing to grant that every airline has "done wrong" by somebody, but is there any way to tell which is the least likely to cause trouble for you?

Most airline passengers consider price and convenience first. If price is no object, they may consider the service provided. Only if there's a crash, or if there's a series of bad headlines, will there be a temporary dip in an airline's reservation orders.

International travelers have some lines they like to rave about. SwissAir, for instance, gets a lot of high marks from people. Singapore Airlines puts on up to eighteen (count 'em!) flight attendants, and Lufthansa gets praised because of its efficiency and the amenities offered.

It takes nothing away from the management of these companies to say that they can offer these comforts because they have an entire country's resources backing them. U.S. air carriers don't have that advantage. Nor, to be frank, do we have a tradition of hand-serving people.

When a U.S. air carrier goes up against a foreign one, the financial considerations can be a bit of an eye-opener. Gone are the lunch meats and the inedible chicken platters and in their place is fine food that even a Frenchman wouldn't quibble over.

On my line's flights to Europe, we offer an international dinner menu. A full first-class meal costs about fifty-two dollars. That's fifty-two dollars that it's costing the *airline*—and that doesn't include wine, and it doesn't include the flight attendants' salaries.

People don't realize just how expensive things get up there. A simple bag of ice costs between five and ten dollars. If we suffer a delay and have to order more ice bags, each additional bag is likely to cost up to twenty dollars!

Of course the average U.S. traveler has an entirely different slant on things. He's far more concerned about fare and about the convenience offered. He's also concerned about the fact that, since deregulation, just getting there by air has become an emotionally draining experience for him.

The only rule of thumb by which to assess U.S. carriers is the degree to which the carrier is either surviving or else not surviving. If it's a profitable line, it will probably do well by you. If it's running in the red, that's likely to come back and bite you sometime.

In making that judgment I feel somewhat regretful. There are unprofitable lines that have some really top people working for them. Their pilots are skilled, their agents are dedicated. They continue to have pride in the line's name and in the tradition behind it.

Nevertheless, all that red ink is killing them. They'll have fewer and older planes, and they're likely to have more maintenance problems. Since the planes they do have are more apt to be gas-guzzlers, they'll have to spend more on fuel, and that will hurt them in other areas.

There are nine major lines currently dominating our air routes. You can practically rate them by their relative profitability. You can put American, Delta, USAir, and Northwest at the top of the list, and you can put Pan Am, Continental, and Eastern in the bottom portion.

United and TWA hover uneasily in the middle somewhere.

This by no means implies that you aren't safe flying a red-ink airline. Continental, Pan Am, and Eastern all have excellent safety records. In fact, Eastern Airlines, for all its notoriety, has one of the better safety records of the deregulation era.

But, as a matter of percentages, you should go where the money is going. When time is of the essence, or when you're trying to make a connection somewhere, you are probably better off flying a line that's making profits. You are more likely to arrive happily, and without feeling that you've been hassled by somebody.

## Chapter 15

# The View from Airplane City

I see by the clock it's almost nine-thirty local time. We are due to arrive at approximately nine fifty-seven. I'm going to radio Center, and we're going to begin our descent now. In another few minutes, we'll begin our approach procedure.

If you were to hand me a map and say, "Point me toward heaven; draw me a circle around the heart of the airplane sentiment," the place that I'd pick would not be Seattle or Kitty Hawk—I'd pick the fifty-mile area surrounding the town we're about to land in now.

In many ways Tucson is a monument to aerospace. To land in this city is to land in Nirvana. At any given time you'll see more airplanes parked here than in any other place in the entire Western Hemisphere.

Near the center of the city, taking up 2,300 acres and harboring pilots and ground crews and rattlesnakes and roadrunners, sprawls a huge tract of land controlled by Davis-Monthon Air Force Base, on which some 2,500 planes are kept in varying degrees of readiness. Most of them are warplanes. They're just sitting there in mothballs. Their intakes are taped. Their windows have dope sprayed over them. Lizards and scorpions make their homes in their wheel wells. Many of these planes go back to before the Vietnam War era.

On a field south of that is the Pima Air Museum. Here, laced with dust, there are about a hundred more airplanes sitting. They're supported by donations from ex-pilots and plane enthusiasts. Old P-38s suffer the indignity of having children gawk at them.

Head thirty miles north, and you'll find the Evergreen Air Center. The Evergreen Air Center is a kind of "chop shop" cum auction block. They'll refit old planes, put new seats and new engines in them, and sell them to the Saudis, or to mercenaries, or to rock performers.

This is something you don't realize if you aren't a member of the airplane crowd. A plane, unlike a car, has an extremely long life expectancy. Even after it's grounded, it will be reused and, eventually, cannibalized. It takes a good number of years before it will return to the dust it sprang from.

An informal count of the area around Tucson may find 3,500 planes, plus various fuselages and tail assemblies. That's as many different planes as belong to all the U.S. airline companies. It's a dry, rust-free world, and it's considered perfect for plane mummification.

Just being in this town brings out the poet and the philosopher in me. The dust smells of oil. The wind whines with turbine noises. As you walk around those planes you can hear the ghosts of dead pilots talking. The emotions you feel are both varied and at odds with each other.

That America means flying almost goes without saying nowadays. We're the Kings of Aviation. There is nobody even close to us. In an economy like ours, ridden with deficits and trade imbalances, our aerospace industry represents a $15 billion annual surplus for us. We may not stay on top. Europe keeps gaining. Japan has become an entry in the supersonic transport sweepstakes. But until the end of this century we will probably remain dominant, and, if we play our cards right, we may be leaders into the next century.

The reason we're on top has some very interesting aspects to it. When the people at Boeing decide to build a new passenger plane, the plane they develop isn't just designed to serve vacation travelers—it is often built in consort with the needs of our Defense Department.

The world in which I live has some very notable warrior overtones. There's a "great chain of being." It often begins in the Pentagon. The instruments and hardware which power today's warplanes will eventually be incorporated into the next decade's passenger planes. There's an advantage to this. Take the Boeing 707. That was developed from a prototype also used for a military tanker. Having mastered the technology under Defense Department auspices (namely for the earlier B-47 and B-52 bombers), Boeing had a tremendous head start in getting it marketed for civilian purposes.

This "great chain of being" makes competitors leery of us. Countries like Japan don't have that military plank to build on. Companies like Airbus, which is subsidized by Europe, must often play catch-up when it comes to our defense technology.

This in no way implies that we will continue to be dominant. With each passing year, we're losing a bit of our market share. The commuter airplane business is now almost totally a foreign business. If you want to buy a commuter, you have to look to Italy or Brazil or someplace.

That notwithstanding, America is the paragon. The defense needs are ours, and so are the civilian demands. There is no other industry currently operating in our society which so vividly represents the so-called "military-industrial complex."

These links to the military aren't just limited to hardware. Many of us pilots are, by training, ex-military pilots. This helps explain why, in an era of feminism, there are fewer than 500 women among our 60,000 airline pilots.

To prepare for this chapter, I made some calls to some woman pilots. I wanted to be sure that my impressions were accurate. What I'm about to say here is but one man's opinion—but it's an opinion that's been tempered by some input across the gender threshold:

Women airline pilots have been increasing in number lately. A few years ago, you wouldn't have even seen any women. If a woman had the urge to be a part of the airline business she'd have had to do so as an agent, or a flight attendant, or a cleaning woman. Today my own company has about thirty women pilots flying. Several of these women have managed to make it to the captain's level. We have not grown so bold as to show their faces in advertising yet, but they are there, and they are prospering, and there are multiplying numbers of them.

There are some very serious obstacles facing the would-be female airline pilot. Equality is fine, so long as you maintain your safety standards. There is nothing inferior about a qualified aviatrix, but she's got several disadvantages when it comes to working in an airline environment.

The first is the fact that she'll be fighting male chauvinism. There's a story they tell that's attributed to American. Having just hired two women, the AAL management decided that henceforth some candidates should have to pass certain strength requirements. The test they devised was a test that used rudder pedals. They required it of all pilots weighing 150 pounds or less. There were six of these pilots, including the two women candidates, and they had to prove their ability to hold the rudder in a Velocity Minimum Control exercise.

The test was set up. It was performed in a simulator. The machinery was programmed for a double left-wing engine failure. When the test was completed, the pilots climbed out again—

—and, lo and behold, the women had done better than some of the men had done!

It is generally agreed that airlines no longer behave that way. Institutionally, at least, they have abandoned their skepticism. They are willing to admit that women are capable and that flying a jet requires no great testosterone level.

But I've had women inform me that, on an informal basis, they are still often 'tested' by dubious flight instructors. 'For some reason,' says one, 'whenever there's a 'hydraulic failure,' it's virtually assured that I'll be the one at the controls at the time.'

A second deterrent is that women are not "military." This is an area that has a good bit more substance going for it. There is a notable distinction between a civilian-trained pilot and one who has spent many, many years flying high-performance military equipment.

The military pilot has had millions of dollars spent on him. He's had many hundreds of hours spent in classrooms and simulator training. He'll have several thousand hours actually spent at high altitude, and if he's been trained to fly fighters, he'll have many, many landing operations.

There are women, of course, who have had the same amount of military training. There isn't an A-10 or a Tomcat that hasn't been flown by a female. But women are proscribed by the laws governing combat. Their numbers are few, and they aren't a top-of-the-list recruiting priority.

This makes it tough when it comes to getting an airline position. The civilian-trained pilot is at a distinct disadvantage here. He (or, in this case, she) will have had to spend a small fortune to attain even the barest of minimums that have been conferred on the military pilot.

In fairness to women, when it comes to this distinction, it may be that some of what we're talking about is really based on male ego problems. I've had women inform me that a lack of military background doesn't bother female pilots so much as it seems to bother the male civilian pilots. However that may be, there's still a distinction there. You'll sometimes hear a pilot say, "I got here the hard way." This is a pilot's way of saying that he made it without the military. It's an intangible kind of thing, but, beneath the pride, there's a defensiveness about it.

The military pilot seems to have a lot more assurance going for him.

You can see it in his walk. You can hear it in the commands he gives you. It's all clipped and clear. He has a coolness, a cockiness about him. There are some great civilian pilots, but they're not up there with the combat heroes.

Unfortunately, right now we're being confronted by a pilot shortage. The modern-day military is offering greatly enhanced pay packages. When a young man signs up, they'll not only send him to college, they'll pay him a handsome monthly wage and offer him a very attractive reenlistment bonus.

This makes it tough on the financially strapped airline companies. Here are these lines, they're in a brutally rough business market, and while their expanded flight structures require them to dig up new pilot talent, many top pilots are saying, "Thanks, but you can't afford us any more."

To compensate for this, we're hiring more and more civilian pilots. There are always civilians who are eager to put on an airline uniform. The only trouble is, some of these civilians aren't well-qualified civilians. Indeed, there has been a noted diminution in "new hires'" training and flying ability.

At the beginning of this book, I mentioned a crash out in Denver. I talked about a Continental pilot who tipped a wing during takeoff. This twenty-six-year-old apprentice had had no jet experience, he had never flown in snow, and he had the salary of a salt-mine worker. Unfortunately, nowadays this is becoming more common. The average "new hire" used to have 2,300 hours of jet experience. In 1988, he had a mere 1,600 hours, and there have been some years of late when that has dropped to as low as 800 hours.

In the sixties and seventies, back at the height of the Vietnam era, the three branches of service were releasing about 4,000 pilots annually. These 4,000 pilots were all trying to become airline pilots, and the airlines were offering only about 1,000 openings a year to them.

As of the time of this writing, we're hiring *10,000* pilots annually. The three service branches are discharging only about 1,500. The other 8,500 have to come from various civilian sources, including air taxis, regionals, cargo planes and commuter services.

Back when I joined up, the competition was incredible. The standards were so high they almost verged on the ludicrous. You couldn't wear glasses. You had to look like Superman. You had to be a college graduate, and it might help to have had a few medals pinned on you.

Today it's more lax. Many companies have lowered their flight requirements. You don't need perfect vision, and you don't have to look like a movie star. They'll let you steer a plane if you're tall enough to see over the glare shield, and you don't even have to be young—they're hiring many middle-aged pilots on some lines.

Don't get me wrong—these can be very fine fliers we're talking about. It's been charged, and is perhaps true, that some of the old rules were arbitrary. There's nothing intrinsically suspect about a pilot who wears glasses, and a five-foot-two woman can handle the controls of most jet equipment.

Nevertheless, it's created some dubiety. There's a feeling afloat that some of the carriers have been "reaching" lately. That pilot who crashed in Denver had been fired by a commuter line, and it was rumored that Texas Air had hired him to become an Eastern Airlines strikebreaker.

Fortunately, the industry has been trying to come to terms with this. Over the last several years, we've begun to develop our own "farm systems." Like the Dodgers or the Yankees, we've been buying up regionals and training regional lines' pilots to take their place in our seniority systems.

We might take this further. Some people have been suggesting that we should start developing pilots while they're still at the high school level. They should be nurtured "from the cradle" to assume command of an airplane, much like Eastern-bloc countries currently nurture their Olympic athletes.

In fact the European lines have long made do with civilian candidates. The pilots at Lufthansa didn't come off old Messerschmidts. They were recruited as civilians and trained as civilians—and, as every pilot knows, they are as good as any of our military pilots.

Subtler than the fact that women face military and chauvinist challenges is that the ambiance in a cockpit is decidedly masculine. The women who fly are the kind who can accept this. There is no way a captain is going to put up with a feminist criticizing him.

The women to whom I've spoken—many of whom have farm backgrounds (aviation, for some reason, isn't attractive to female city dwellers)—say that the two biggest errors a woman can make are to (a) try to "prove something," and (b) try to be "buddy-buddy." As one woman put it: "I'm in this for the love it. I'm not 'one of the guys,' and I don't even pretend to be. What I am is a *pilot*. After a while men appreciate that. They may have to change their language, but eventually they get comfortable with me."

Her assessment seems apt. When you're far out over the Atlantic, and it's two in the morning, and there's nothing but the stars surrounding you, the talk on the flight deck can turn determinedly "manly." The humor gets crass. The memories are often hair-raising.

Some of these guys are, in my opinion, saintly. They'll tell stories about Korea that will literally make your blood curdle. They'll have been imprisoned in Hanoi. They'll have penetrated Cambodia. To me it's an honor just to share the same flight deck with them.

There are critics, of course, who have doubts about this ambiance. A few years ago, I saw a British TV documentary. It showed a bunch of young employees from People Express Airline, and these employees were all enthusing over PEA's management program.

People, you'll recall, had a "commune"-type management style. Flight crews and baggage handlers acted more or less interchangeably. A Seven-Four captain might arrive at an airport, step off the plane, and immediately start filling in as a scheduling agent.

These employees were bubbly. "It's just great!" they said, starry-eyed. "What makes it so great is that we have none of that military stuff! Our guys in the cockpit are just the same as our ground crew members! We're all one big family! We're the wave of the future!" they said confidently.

Well, the answer to that has been delivered by history. People Express couldn't last out the price war era. In 1986 they were bought by Frank Lorenzo, and all those young, fresh-faced kids are flying freight or working in a gas station somewhere.

But the thing that got to me were those remarks about the military. It's hard for me to imagine any philosophy more wrongheaded. There may be many fine venues for "democratic management," but the deck of a jet is most assuredly not one of them.

When I get on a plane, I like to know what I'm dealing with. With a military man, I know his behavior will be predictable. I know how he thinks. I know how he responds to things. Above all, I know whether his flight log is accurate or not.

If it's a civilian on deck, I'm a little more leery of him. I can't be that sure of just who it is that I'm dealing with. He says he's flown a JetStar. Maybe he *has* flown a JetStar. Or maybe he had a friend who was just willing to say he had flown a JetStar at one point.

We've been talking in this book about "Cockpit Resource Management." Basically what that means is that we're looking at the human element. We get in a simulator, we run through a flight operation, and we videotape ourselves. Then we look at the way we performed together.

It's amazing what we'll see. We'll see captains snub crew members. We'll see two men gang up and form a "cabal" against a third pilot. We'll see

162

gruff, teasing humor which is meant to be funny, but which cuts off dissent and often quells the advice that's being given.

One of the most incredibly inane accidents in the history of our industry was a United DC-8 that had to crash-land in Oregon. The captain was a war horse who for the final half-hour kept ignoring crewmen's advice that they had almost no fuel reserves left. As far as the captain was concerned, he was the king of that cockpit. He was busy being "in charge," and he was concerned about a landing gear problem. Eventually, the plane suffered a triple engine flameout. It crashed into some woods, carrying 189 people with it.

From this we may deduce that we have too many "iron pants" up there. We have too many graduates of the Clint Eastwood Flying Academy. They'll take no advice, and they'll brook no interference; as far as they're concerned, everyone else is there to get coffee for them.

I've known such pilots. I had a superior back in the seventies once. He was an Errol Flynn type who liked to fraternize with passengers. He'd take the plane up, say, "Okay, kid, you steer it," then disappear in back and spend twenty or thirty minutes back there.

There sat yours truly. I'd be sitting with my oxygen mask on. There's an FAA rule about flying at high altitude: If you're alone in the cockpit, and you're at 24,000 feet or over, you have to put on a mask in case you suddenly lose your cabin pressure.

The only trouble is, those damn masks can get muggy sometimes. After twenty or thirty minutes they start making your face perspire. That captain, God bless him, was flirting with the ladies, and there sat his flunky sucking air through a hose apparatus.

One day I gave up. I radioed our control center. I asked for an altitude below 24,000 feet. I had barely nosed over and begun to lower the airplane when the flight-deck door opened and there was the captain behind me.

*"What the hell are you doing?"*

"I'm flying," I said to him.

*"Where the hell is your mask?"* (By now I had taken the oxygen mask off.)

"Don't sweat it," I told him. "We're at 23,000 feet now. I'll keep flying the plane, and you can go back and continue socializing."

I don't advise making a habit of talking to your superior that way, but at least, in this case, it got him to sit in the cockpit again.

Despite such transgressions, I'll cast my lot with the military guys. I'd rather deal with ego than with a person who lacks the training skills. You can teach a John Wayne to be as sensitive as Woody Allen, but you can't teach a Woody Allen to take command when your wings are burning.

The people who become pilots are, in a way, predisposed to flying. They've usually been attracted since the time they were teenagers. They're invariably intelligent and, for the most part, adventurous. They're attracted to flying because of its speed and because of its daring attributes.

These are not the kind of people to whom you look to advance social causes. They are highly competitive. They may not be that "liberal-minded." Many of these guys can be irritatingly prejudiced—but I wouldn't trade a one of them for a room full of college professors.

What's troubling to me is that, lacking the military, we're hiring civilians with more dubious preparatory backgrounds. We're putting them quickly into a two-man cockpit, which gives them a very crucial role in the handling of the flight equipment. When I was coming up, you started off as a flight engineer. You had already been military, and you might have had a very high command position; but when you came to the airlines you had to start at the bottom again. And it was several long years before they'd turn a control yoke over to you.

People sometimes ask me, "What kind of flying do you prefer? Since you obviously admire the Air Force and Navy types, it's natural to wonder why you gave up the service and committed yourself to a lifetime of passenger complaints."

I have an answer to that, and it may be surprising to you: There is simply no comparison between civilian and military flying. If your love is to *fly*, then you have to stay military. That's a very special world—both in the thrills and in the glory department.

Consider the power. You're sitting in a fighter jet. You have a big enough engine to pulverize the sound barrier. You have enough destructive force to wipe out a city. You have a mission to run, and you have very few restraints to hinder you. That's extremely heady stuff. You can feel the adrenaline. You pull that stick back, and you suck it hard in your midsection. You lift your nose up and you head straight for the stratosphere. You're flying with eagles, and you have the feeling of godhead within you.

Flying an airliner is like driving a tour bus. The name of the game is maturity and stability. I've known many Top Guns who can't hack it in the airline business. They don't have the patience—they're simply too full of rebelliousness.

But, oh God, the Corps. . . . Don't talk to me about passenger delays. There's a tank on the hill. Your job is to neutralize it. You scream in to earth with your afterburners roaring, and if you don't hit the tank, you can at least blow the hill out from under it. Talk about sex—that is the true aphrodisiac. And when you come in to land, you always land like a bandit's chasing you. You drop like a loon, making streaks on the runway, and so what if it's rough, you don't have any little old ladies to worry about.

Disapprove all you want, that's how a guy like me feels about it. Don't get me wrong, I appreciate the job I have; but if it weren't for the security and the lifestyle I'm used to, I'd go back in a minute. And so would two out of three other airline pilots.

We're about to come in now. We've got the gear and the wing flaps lowered. Fasten your belts. Please extinguish all smoking material. Those mountains you see are the Catalinas to the north of us. Those are the Rincons straight ahead, and those are the Sierritas to the left down there. Coming into Tucson is usually a relatively easy landing procedure. There's never any snow. There's rarely any rain to speak of. There are times—not too many—when the wind can get tricky, but it doesn't top the list of anyone's most dreaded U.S. airports.

When we get off this plane, it's going to fly on to Seattle. Now Seattle's a place that gets some very bad weather conditions. You can have peasoupers up there that are like something out of Dickens. Seattle's Sea-Tac International has some of our most advanced landing equipment.

I'd like to tell you about that, and about our "zero-zero" landings in which the fog is so thick it's like a blanket of mud in front of you, and when you come in to land you've got your plane set on "autoland," and you can't see a thing until you actually feel the runway hitting you. I'd like to tell you about that, only it would probably just scare you. Even in the cockpit one can feel a certain tension mounting. It's not caused by worry—it's caused by . . . well, by *irrelevance,* possibly. The machines are in control, and you feel completely superfluous to them. Of course, most of our landings are reliant on instruments nowadays. The lack of visibility is but an unwonted psychic factor. As a modern airline pilot you learn to trust electronics and be more or less skeptical of what you're seeing through that glass in front of you.

But there's a certain heady drama in a completely blind airplane landing. It can only be done in certain planes and at certain landing facilities. And as you drop through the mist you hear the sound of your warning tone, and the next sound you'll hear is the sound of the runway under you.

I'd like to take you through that, only here it's all sunshine. We're three miles away, and we've got no visibility problems. Our flight director system shows that we are aligned with the runway, and we've got another signal showing that we've got a fix on the glide slope now. It's still a busy time. It's here you came in, remember. I'm looking at my airspeed. I'm cross-checking my attitude gauge. To round this book off, I'd like to bring it in smoothly. After all, that's how 99.99 percent of our landings are done nowadays.

## Chapter 16

# **F**lying into the Twenty-first Century

That pretty much explains what it's like to be an airline pilot. I've probably managed to disenchant a few of you. For others, no doubt, I've only further mythologized it. That's the thing about my job—even the bad parts sound good to some people.

What remains to be asked is where these currents are taking us. Are we headed, as some fear, toward a major catastrophe? Or are we about to break through into a new, golden era in which we travel more safely for lower fares and with better passenger service?

When I was young, growing up, back in the quaint 1950s, I'd gaze at magazine pictures of what the world of the eighties would look like. I'd see rocket-shaped automobiles and flying-saucer airplanes and sleek, spiraling roads that grazed the tips of gold skyscrapers. The people in those pictures were always happy and had smiles on their faces. Why shouldn't they be smiling? Technology had solved everything for them. It never seemed to occur that, along with spaceships and monorails, there would be poverty and drug abuse and terrorism and water pollution.

The next dozen years are going to see advances in the airline industry.

Some will be small; some will be notable. By the early 2000s we'll be looking at advancements which, by present-day standards, will seem absolutely incredible to us.

The business itself will have changed quite remarkably. Inevitably, I think, we'll see many fewer airline companies. One of the most ironic results of our current deregulation is that, instead of promoting competition, it has strengthened our oligopolistic tendencies.

Nevertheless, we are going to see advances. I have every expectation that the future will get brighter for us. We've already seen improvements just in the last couple of years that make the early 1980s seem comparatively primitive to us.

Along with the advancements, there will also be some negative currents. Because of economics, there are increasing amounts of pressure on us. There's a feeling in the air that you have to improve it or else eliminate it; if you can't do either one, then you've got try to wring more productivity out of it.

You may have read recently about the problems of cockpit fatigue. I alluded to this earlier when I talked about the schedules we're keeping. We're flying more hours, with ever-diminishing rest periods, and we're compressing more work into increasingly condensed time-frames.

It's been estimated recently that for every hour of flight time, pilots spend at least one additional hour in duty-related ground time. While we enjoy flexibility, we aren't getting the rest we need. Our total working hours are beginning to rival an office worker's hours.

These schedules are such that even our rest has grown restless. Our days may be separated by inadequate sleep periods. We'll take off around midnight, we'll have three or four legs to fly, and we'll land around noon and have to sleep while the sun is still shining.

This "backside-of-the-clock" flying is beginning to tell on us physically. With our advanced, electric cockpits, much of our job is a monitoring job. We run ever-increasing dangers of becoming hypnotized, forgetful of things. We have to guard against "microsleep," in which we doze with our eyes still open.

There have been several serious episodes directly attributable to pilot fatigue. There was a Boston-bound jet whose captain fell asleep during a landing procedure. There was a China Airlines plane which went into a nosedive after its completely bushed crew relied too heavily on its autopilot features. This is something not appreciated by our comptrollers and profit-watchers. They'll say, "Aw, c'mon, guys—you're carrying an eighty-hour work month, aren't you?" and they'll completely miss the point that our work is not like their work, and that we can never drop our guard or spend a second with our minds unfocused.

Traditionally, of course, it was the planes that were the weak point. If you overtaxed the plane, you could bend, or even break it possibly. The men on the flight deck always worried about pushing, lest the engines stop running, or the wings start to disintegrate on them. Today, if there's a failure, it's more likely to be a *human* failure. Before the wings go, you're more likely to feel your retinas detach. And, what with all the computers, we're behind the curve mentally. We have to redesign planes to help us overcome our attentiveness shortcomings.

There's an idea in the works called *random interrogation.* We're beginning to design systems that are made to act as gadflies to us. They'll ask pilots questions that the pilots must answer so that the machine will be satisfied that it's got a mentally alert companion flying with it. We're also considering systems that require more *mandatory position reporting.* It's not that our centers don't know where we are up there; but by making the pilot report and declare himself, it will keep him alert and help to prevent his attention from wandering.

To give you the drift of where our thinking is taking us: I was recently at a meeting in which we were brainstorming new flight procedures. The suggestion was given that we ought to utilize our flight attendants better. We ought to have them come up and help break up the monotony for us.

I won't regale you here with how this meeting disintegrated. Suffice it to say that there was a debate about bust measurements. The idea of using women to help us spark up our brain cells was a novel idea that was not lost on the male pilot group.

But this points up the fact that we're fighting human frailty. We're too disengaged. We are not equipped to be monitors. The next generation's planes will be even smarter than our present airplanes, and we need newer, fresher ways to keep ahead of all those computers they'll have on them.

Many newer planes are being designed to have sleep compartments. These are Pullman-like berths in which a crewman can refresh himself. On transoceanic flights you'll have three qualified pilots, but only two will be flying while one is resting in the sleep compartment.

Some of these designs can give you an almost claustrophobic feeling. We're getting closer and closer to becoming long-distance truck drivers. It may be common in the nineties to have fourteen-hour flight legs where we won't even have the luxury of putting down to get a crew replacement.

That's bad enough, but you passengers will suffer. The economics are such that no line can afford to increase passenger comfort. Although advances are being made in both seat design and storage space, each advance is being offset by our need to stuff more bodies in there.

There have been some interesting concepts that are being dreamed about by airplane builders. Airbus has a plan that will utilize freight containers. An overseas passenger will simply vacate his passenger seat, enter the hold, and take a snooze in a freight container. McDonnell Douglas wants cabins that are modular. The passengers will board via a lounge in the terminal. The entire cabin section will be wheeled to the airplane, where it will be loaded, full of passengers, through a wide-opening nose portal.

All this is great, but it is also impractical. What we're really going to get are more seats and less passenger room. Even the overhead compartments (which would be designed for the purpose, obviously) might be used to hold stewardesses who are on rest breaks or on assignment changes.

The airplanes themselves will, of course, be sophisticated. Interestingly, many of them will show a return to propeller engines. There's a new kind of jet that uses multi-fan propellers and consumes about half as much fuel as the conventional jet turbine uses.

We'll also see planes that use a new kind of instrument display. Called "heads-up" display, it was created for our military. All the readings you need are displayed across your windscreen, so that you won't lose a second lowering your eyes to look at your instrument panel.

Infrared scanning . . . traffic alert and collision avoidance systems . . . on-board windshear warnings . . . sophisticated data terminals . . . It's going to be harder and harder to have an old-fashioned airplane accident. Which, of course, will compel us to start coming up with *new* kinds of accidents.

We're seeing more and more mistakes that are actually attributable to technology. As technology increases, so do complacency and "hi-tech overload." We're becoming dangerously reliant on our sophisticated hardware, and we can sometimes make mistakes that will seem ridiculous to the average nonexpert.

There have been instances of pilots who have forgotten to take their wheel brakes off. I know—that's absurd. But I can assure you it's possible. You can be roaring down a runway, being propelled by your engines, and suddenly, to your surprise, you hear a bang, and it's your tires exploding.

There have been instances of pilots who have forgotten to lock a cockpit window. The window can be closed, but it still won't have the latch turned properly. You can be rolling down the runway at about 160 knots and have the window fly open and suddenly you're confronted with a cyclone in there.

We have yet to invent the cockpit that can anticipate all the mistakes we can make. You can be about to take off and forget to start one of your engines up. If it's a three-engine Tri-Star, you can be closing on your V speed and be about to leave the ground and have a third of your power missing.

The engineer's answer is simply to eliminate the human factor. That's clear enough; after all, we're the dunces, aren't we? It only makes sense to turn the plane into a robot. You can fly it like a drone. You can use one of those boxes with a control rod sticking out of it.

The only problem is, these planes aren't like space rockets. We are not firing missiles into an eventless, black vacuum. We are transporting real people through an ever-changing atmosphere, and only a pilot who's there can make the incredibly fast decisions that are needed.

Sometimes our companies have a hard time remembering this. Back in the pre-dereg days, most of our executives had pilot experience. They knew, all too well, that in real-life operations only the man at the stick could tell whether a storm cloud was penetrable or not. Not so today. Most of our executives are business people. They've been reared as accountants, or lawyers, or fast-food experts. The people in operations have been moved from the power center; they've lost much of their say over our personnel and even our procurement policies.

I tell you these things not because I feel overly pessimistic about it. On the contrary, I don't. We're going to survive and grow stronger probably. But it's important that our vision be clear and realistic. We won't always be happy in the ultra-efficient world we're building.

Having recognized that, we can look to some positives. There are things coming up which will probably be wonderful. All we have to do is get our money and our priorities in order and we will soon have a system that will make the present look primitive to us.

One great advance will be the *microwave landing system.* MLS, as we call it, will replace our present-day landing systems. Today, when we land, we have to line up on the centerline and follow the same approach profile as the planes behind us and in front of us are following.

The microwave system uses an entirely different landing method. Beams are shot out in the shape of a three-dimensional pie wedge. Planes can come in following either straight or curved glide slopes, approaching from all different directions and using a variety of different descent gradients.

You can imagine how this will augment the efficiency of some of our more congested airports.

As I mentioned before, we have air traffic control problems. The computers they're using are out of the age of transistors. The blips that are appearing on those porthole-shaped radarscopes are being illuminated by means of hard-wired panels and vacuum tubes.

Replacing this equipment is part of our National Airspace System Plan. This is a multi-billion-dollar plan designed to rejuvenate our traffic system. In the past it's been stalled because of our federal budget deficit problems, but it will get here eventually, and when it does it will make life easier for us.

At the FAA Tech Center they have an enormous computer testing laboratory. It's the largest in the world; it's the size of two football fields. It has row after row of sophisticated mainframes that are due to take their place in all our towers and in our control centers.

These computers won't work by means of signals fed by ground radar. Instead, they'll draw signals from a matrix of space satellites. Every plane aloft will be tracked via satellite, and when there's talking to be done, it will be done via a computer terminal.

Wired to these computers will be multi-screened "sector suites." These will take the place of the controllers' round radarscopes. They'll show much more information than is presently being transmitted, and, through Datalink transmission, we'll have greatly reduced radio jam-ups.

Of course none of this matters if we don't have more airport space. That's a common enough gripe. I imagine it's familiar to you. Ask any expert what we're most in dire need of and the first thing he'll tell you is that what we need is more concrete out there.

I recently saw an article in a New York City newspaper. It talked about a $3 billion plan to renovate that area's major airports. The size of this project is, by all accounts, mind-boggling. I pass this along so that you can appreciate the enormity of it:

By the late 1990s, New York's three major airports will have 120 million people annually arriving or leaving from them. That's half the population of the entire United States, wielding handbags and golf clubs and dog carriers and baby strollers. To accommodate this madness, they'll need new airport transit systems. They'll need elevated trains and wider roads and moving people conveyors. They'll need newer, longer runways, more computers, all new baggage scanners, underground fuel lines, and greatly expanded passenger terminals.

And that's just the fields—it doesn't count all the access highways. None of New York's airports is even linked to a subway system. They're going to have twice as many passengers leaving in 50 percent more airplanes, but even for $3 billion they haven't devised a way to transport them there.

Now you can't help but wonder, *Where the hell are all these people going? What's so important that we can't just stay home some evening?* Clearly, we're in an age of unprecedented mobility. Nothing in our past has even remotely prepared us for it.

We have an air system now that's like our roads of forty years ago. You'll recall that back then we had a rural-route highway system. Following World War II, when gas became available again, we were suddenly confronted with rush hours and traffic snafus.

Our solution to that was the Interstate Highway System. This was an enormously expensive program that required a great deal of federal planning. We had to be willing to sacrifice certain local autonomies so that the roads that we built could be laid out and joined up efficiently.

That's where we stand with our present-day air system. Each of our airports is the equivalent of a cloverleaf. Unfortunately, at present we're still stuck in the position of having to go beg the locals and ask if we can put a new off-ramp in there.

The locals, of course, will respond as they always respond. They'll tell us to go jump—they don't want any more airport traffic. From their point of view, their airport seems adequate. So what if it's too small to serve our nationwide travel needs?

What the locals don't realize is that we're dependent upon air travel. According to a poll taken in 1987, three out of four Americans say that we greatly need to expand our air system. Almost one out of four thinks that this should be a high-priority White House item.

We're doing what we can to build quieter, bigger flying machines. Our 757s have extremely low noise emissions. They hold 20 percent more people than our noisy 727s, and that helps to reduce takeoffs and cuts down on noise and on air traffic congestion.

But we'll continue to have trouble as long as we're captive to what the locals want. Our airports are being treated like our prisons and our homeless shelters. Everybody knows that we need a hell of a lot more of them, but no one has the leadership to counteract the intense resistance to them.

One possible option is to build what might be called "superports." These would be huge, sprawling airports far removed from our population centers. They could be strategically located, three or four across the country, and they'd be fed by many routes leading from the surrounding geographical areas. Our present city airports could be converted to become commuter airports. We could ferry city passengers via newly designed "tiltrotors." These are experimental planes which can lift off like helicopters, then downtilt their engines and continue to fly like a conventional airplane.

That's one solution. It may be a simplistic one. The trouble with airports is that they are little like McDonald's franchises. Once one goes in, you've got the beginnings of a metropolis. You'd have to have very strict zoning not to create new congestion areas.

From a global perspective, things are equally complicated. What we're seeing at present is a shift in the marketplace. The "Pacific Rim" area, from Taiwan to Australia, may soon replace Europe as our most lucrative passenger market.

At present, the Orient represents about $10 billion annually to us. We're carrying 10 million passengers each year to various Rim countries. These figures should increase by about 10 percent annually, and may actually quadruple by the time the year 2000 gets here.

To service this area involves a number of difficulties. We have great logistic problems. We can't always get spare parts that easily. If an airplane breaks down and has to be fixed in Korea, we may have to send clear to Bangkok in order to locate the part that's needed.

From a flight crew's perspective, it can sometimes get dicey. We don't know the languages. We don't know the rules they play by. Try as we might, we continue to make *faux pas.* There are a dozen different cultures, and they don't always agree with one another.

There's a story going around that's attributed to United. United has been opening a number of Pacific Rim air routes lately. In a spirit of good will, they put new uniforms on their agents and had them stand at all their counters wearing jackets with white carnations in them.

What United didn't realize, because no one had told them, was that, to people of Asian background, white carnations are a bad luck symbol. So here were these agents standing around at the airports, and the passengers they were greeting felt like they were going to a funeral ceremony.

There is a story, equally typical, about an airline flying to Australia. On their in-flight magazine they ran a picture of Paul Hogan ("Crocodile Dundee"). All well and good, only they inadvertently accompanied it with a headline that contained a slang word that, in Australian, stood for sex perversion.

You can say a lot of things about Crocodile Dundee, mate, but you don't call him a pervert.

Flights being pricey, there's an emphasis on passenger service. A trans-Pacific fare can cost up to $6,000 nowadays. Your meal may be served on the finest bone china and consist of caviar and steak, plus *pâtè en croûte*, with a little Chardonnay to finish it.

I wouldn't look for that to be the policy indefinitely. Once we're locked in, we'll become ever more economy-minded. We're stressing service now because those high fares are regulated. If the controls come off fares, we'll have a quick return to Spartanism.

Despite all these problems, our lines want those route assignments. The six biggest airlines see the Pacific as pivotal. Cargo alone has become a multi-billion-dollar business. And, of course, we all lick our chops over the potential of the China market.

The lure of these treasures is beginning to awaken our science fantasies. After years of inactivity we're beginning to plan for SSTs again. You'll remember that in the seventies we rejected supersonics and placed serious restraints on the British-French Concorde's land overflights.

But the growth of the Pacific puts a whole different cast on everything. To reach Japan quickly becomes more than just a novelty; it's also got the impetus of dollars and cents behind it. And vast, teeming China offers an even greater financial incentive.

One thing we've learned: When we go supersonic, we're going to have to build planes that are a lot bigger than the Concorde is. To get the fares down to where people can afford them, we're going to have to build planes that are at least as big as our present widebodies.

This isn't easy. Such planes guzzle jet fuel. Their skins virtually fry under the supersonic air friction. They'll require all new technology, including a lot of advanced research, and that makes them too expensive for any of our present private companies to gamble on.

There are three possible scenarios that our industry is looking at. Each of the scenarios represents a stage of technology. The easier the technology, the lower the price tag; the simpler the plane, the sooner it can go into flight testing.

*1. By the year 2005, we could build a Mach 2 widebody.* This would fly 300 passengers at about 1,350 miles per hour. It could fly from New York to London in about three and a half hours, and it would have more than enough range to fly to all the Pacific Rim countries.

*2. If we disregard that, we could develop a Mach 3 airplane.* This plane could be ready by about 2010. It could fly New York-London in under two and a half hours, and it could get us to Japan in just under four hours.

*3. If that's not sufficient, we could gamble on a "leapfrog strategy." We could jump to the future and build a Mach 5 spaceplane.* This could fly us

175

to Tokyo in about two and a half hours, and it would run on liquid hydrogen, which would make it safer for the ozone layer.

Playing these options is what we hire politicians for. Japan has expressed interest. The Europeans are at the card table. It's a high stakes gamble in which the loser could face bankruptcy . . . or, avoiding that pitfall, we could agree to do some resource sharing.

However that evolves, I won't be around to have to worry about it. I'll have hung up my stripes and be in the ground, or else out fishing somewhere. A pilot my age has about ten years of service left. Once you've reached sixty, you're facing mandatory retirement statutes.

But I have a pretty good idea of what these spaceplanes will look like. They'll have long, dartlike bodies with delta-shaped foils attached to them. They'll look something like the planes we used to sail when we were school kids. And as for speed, they'll be fast—but they won't be very comfortable for you.

The first thing you'll note is that there won't be any windows to look out. You can't afford windows on a hypersonic spaceplane. You'll be traveling too fast and at too high an altitude. You'll be at about 100,000 feet, and you'll have severe radiation bombardment.

You'll be stacked cheek by jowl like so many pieces of cordwood. There will be very little freedom. You may barely be allowed bathroom time. What refreshments you get will be stored in your seatback. The back of the seat will be both vendor and entertainment center for you.

When you set down in Tokyo, you'll have immense circadian rhythm problems. You'll be lunching in Japan, but your body will be in Arkansas. If you're a high-powered business traveler, you may be coming right home again. After a few days of that, your body will wonder what the hell you've been doing to it.

When I talk to other pilots, we all laugh about the "space suit problem." This will be a problem they'll have to tackle in the marketing department. It's just one of those little details that the futurists never tell you about. It's going to pit our safety research against the ad boys and the image makers.

On a traditional airliner, we already have oxygen masks. If we're piloting a plane, and it's at 41,000 feet or over, someone in the cockpit has to be wearing an oxygen mask. Should we suddenly lose pressure, we wouldn't have time to get those masks adjusted.

Well, imagine what could happen when you're flying at 100,000 feet. There, if you decompress, you're going to need a full-sized space suit around you. If you don't have a space suit, you're going to expire instantaneously. If you do have a space suit, you might at least keep the plane from crashing.

How will you feel, if you're sitting on a spaceplane, snuggled in your seat with your drink and your television, and here comes this crewman who has to go use the lavatory, and as he tromps through the plane he's got a space suit and a space helmet on? Are you ready for that? Will it make you uneasy? Will it perhaps make you wonder if this airline has its priorities in order? The alternative, of course, is to make *everyone* wear space suits. Won't that be a hit with those finicky New York passengers!

The history of transportation follows the same time-worn cycles. The original object is to get you where you're trying to go. Achieving that object is considered a triumph—whether it's by litter or by cart or by some vehicle that needs fuel to power it. Once that's achieved, we try to increase the comfort factor. We add cushions and tassels and linens and dining service. We emulate kings who are borne by their servants and who bump across deserts eating peeled grapes their eunuchs feed them.

But soon that wears thin. Even luxury grows tiring. Hungry souls itch. We want to get where we're going sooner. We'll give up our grapes and we'll turn in our eunuchs if we can get there by train, or by car, or by unicycle, if it cuts our travel time.

It's the history of man—and it's the history of the airline business. We turn in old glories—and then we look back nostalgically at them. We greet each new cycle full of hope and astonishment, but as we rush to the future we have the feeling that we're losing something.

Sometimes, like now, in this Arizona desert, walking among cactus and looking at all these old airplane relics, I'll entertain fancies of the year 2020 when the planes we're now flying will be sitting where these hulks are sitting. Over there, by that saguaro, there will be a huge, ghostly Boeing. It will be a 747. It will have its intakes and exhaust ports covered. It will be squatting in the sagebrush with its dolphin-like cranium, and there will be a hundred or so tourists standing around and taking snapshots of it.

The tour will commence. They'll enter through the tail section. "How quaint!" they'll all murmur. The air will be mote-ridden. The guide, dressed in plastic, will run through her patter, and they'll hear about the plane and all the many great people who flew her.

As they drift toward the front, they'll be struck by the grandeur of it. All those "earthtone decors" . . . all those seats with real upholstery on them! And look—lookee there! Those are *windows*—real *glass*, by golly! How long has it been since you've seen an airplane with real windows in it?

And now, toward the front, they'll see the *pièce de résistance*. They'll

177

gather up close. The tour guide will silence them. She'll pause for a moment, and then she'll smile at the children, and she'll direct their attention to the structure now facing them.

"And of course," she'll say, beaming, "back in the twentieth century they could afford to have luxuries such as planes with real staircases in them"—and she'll run one smooth hand along that sleek spiral banister, and the tourists will gawk and strain their necks toward the passenger lounge. "Up there," she'll inform them, "is where the first-class passengers sat. They could order mixed drinks. They'd have real, live stewardesses serving them. It's recorded in legend that some of those lounges had pianos in them. Of course those were all gone by the time Frank Lorenzo sold them. . . ."

Incredible! Impossible! It's like a tour of the *Hindenburg!* It's like the *Orient Express,* with its paneling and its flower vases! What a wonderful thing to have lived in that era and to have been able to travel in the lap of such wantonness!

And there will stand the children. This will completely astonish them. They'll be hearing strange words, such as "radio" and "air traffic controller." And it will all run together along with other famous vehicles, such as the *Niña* and the *Pinta* and whatever the *Spirit of St. Louis* was.

"And how long," one might ask, "did it take to fly to Tokyo?"

"Oh, *that,*" says the tour guide. "Well, I guess it took a day or two."

A day or two!

*Gosh!*

How on earth did people live back then?

And with that they'll file out. They're due for dinner in Seoul that evening.